Disney Theatrical Productions
under the direction of
Thomas Schumacher
presents

Disney **Aladdin**
BROADWAY'S NEW MUSICAL COMEDY

Music by	*Lyrics by*	*Book by*
ALAN MENKEN	HOWARD ASHMAN	CHAD BEGUELIN
	TIM RICE and CHAD BEGUELIN	

Based on the Disney film written by RON CLEMENTS, JOHN MUSKER, TED ELLIOTT & TERRY ROSSIO and directed and produced by JOHN MUSKER & RON CLEMENTS

Starring
ADAM JACOBS

JAMES MONROE IGLEHART   COURTNEY REED

BRIAN GONZALEZ   BRANDON O'NEILL   JONATHAN SCHWARTZ

CLIFTON DAVIS   DON DARRYL RIVERA

MERWIN FOARD   MICHAEL JAMES SCOTT

and

JONATHAN FREEMAN

as "Jafar"

TIA ALTINAY MIKE CANNON ANDREW CAO LAURYN CIARDULLO JOSHUA DELA CRUZ
YUREL ECHEZARRETA DAISY HOBBS DONALD JONES, JR. ADAM KAOKEPT NIKKI LONG STANLEY MARTIN
BRANDT MARTINEZ MICHAEL MINDLIN RHEA PATTERSON BOBBY PESTKA KHORI MICHELLE PETINAUD
ARIEL REID JENNIFER RIAS TRENT SAUNDERS JAZ SEALEY DENNIS STOWE MARISHA WALLACE BUD WEBER

Associate Producer	*Technical Supervision*	*Production Supervisor*
ANNE QUART	GEOFFREY QUART/	CLIFFORD SCHWARTZ
	HUDSON THEATRICAL ASSOCIATES	

General Managers	*Associate Director*	*Associate Choreographer*	*Casting*
MYRIAH BASH	SCOTT TAYLOR	JOHN MacINNIS	TARA RUBIN CASTING
EDUARDO CASTRO			ERIC WOODALL, CSA

Dance Music Arrangements	*Music Coordinator*	*Fight Direction*	*Production Stage Manager*
GLEN KELLY	HOWARD JOINES	J. ALLEN SUDDETH	JIMMIE LEE SMITH

Sound Design	*Hair Design*	*Makeup Design*	*Illusion Design*
KEN TRAVIS	JOSH MARQUETTE	MILAGROS MEDINA-CERDEIRA	JIM STEINMEYER

Costume Design	*Lighting Design*
GREGG BARNES	NATASHA KATZ

Scenic Design
BOB CROWLEY

Orchestrations
DANNY TROOB

Music Supervision
Incidental Music & Vocal Arrangements
MICHAEL KOSARIN

Directed and Choreographed by
CASEY NICHOLAW

The premiere of *Aladdin* was produced by The 5th Avenue Theatre in Seattle, WA. David Armstrong, Executive Producer & Artistic Director;
Bernadine C. Griffin, Managing Director; Bill Berry, Producing Director.

Disney characters and artwork © Disney Enterprises, Inc.
Cover Artwork © Disney
Production photos by Deen van Meer
Additional photos by Matthew Murphy and Cylla von Tiedemann

ISBN 978-1-4803-9668-5

Walt Disney Music Company
Wonderland Music Company, Inc.

DISTRIBUTED BY

HAL•LEONARD®
CORPORATION
7777 W. BLUEMOUND RD. P.O. BOX 13819 MILWAUKEE, WI 53213

In Australia Contact:
Hal Leonard Australia Pty. Ltd.
4 Lentara Court
Cheltenham, Victoria, 3192 Australia
Email: ausadmin@halleonard.com.au

Visit Hal Leonard Online at
www.halleonard.com

JAMES MONROE IGLEHART

Arabian Nights

DON DARRYL RIVERA, JONATHAN FREEMAN

ADAM JACOBS, COURTNEY REED

ADAM JACOBS

ADAM JACOBS, COURTNEY REED

ARABIAN NIGHTS

Music by ALAN MENKEN
Lyrics by HOWARD ASHMAN

Misterioso

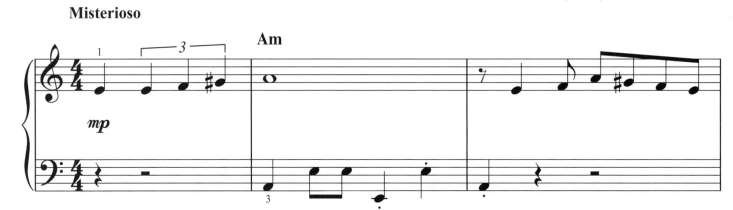

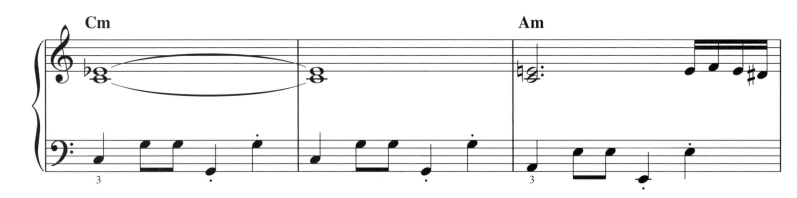

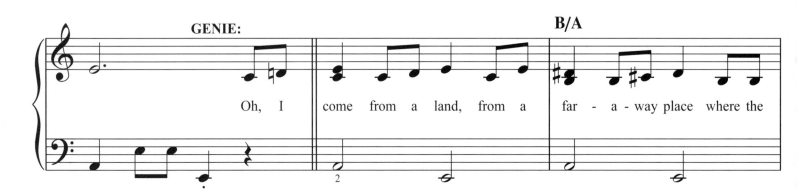

Oh, I come from a land, from a far - a - way place where the

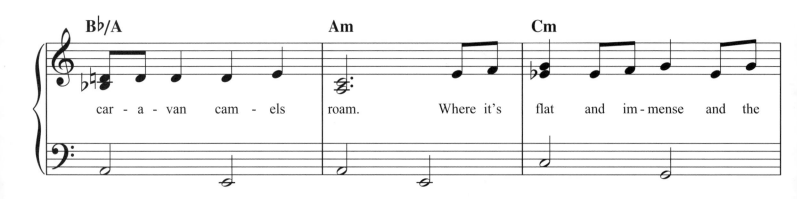

car - a - van cam - els roam. Where it's flat and im - mense and the

heat is in-tense. It's bar-bar-ic, but hey, it's home. When the

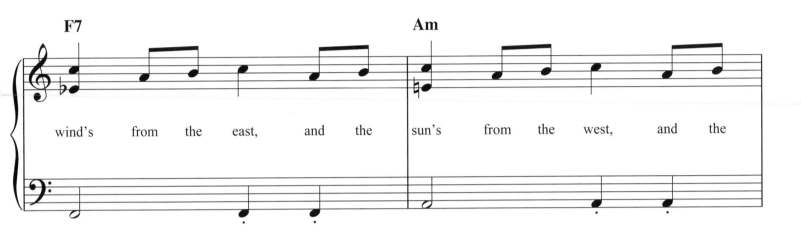

wind's from the east, and the sun's from the west, and the

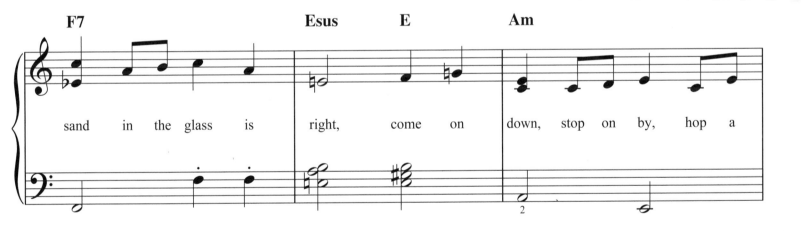

sand in the glass is right, come on down, stop on by, hop a

car-pet and fly to an-oth-er A-ra-bi-an night! _____

Fol - low me to a place where in -

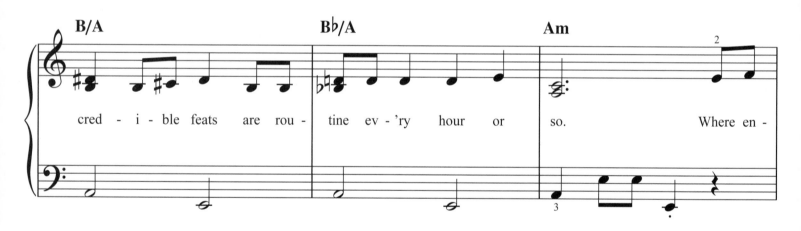

cred - i - ble feats are rou - tine ev - 'ry hour or so. Where en -

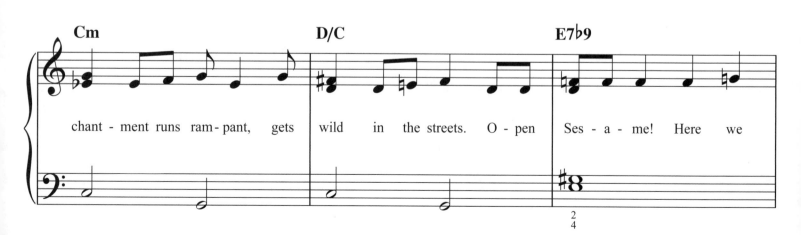

chant - ment runs ram - pant, gets wild in the streets. O - pen Ses - a - me! Here we

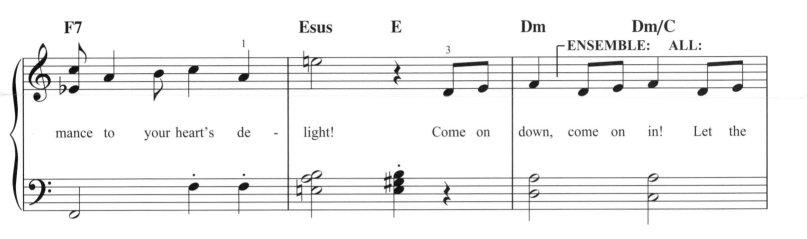

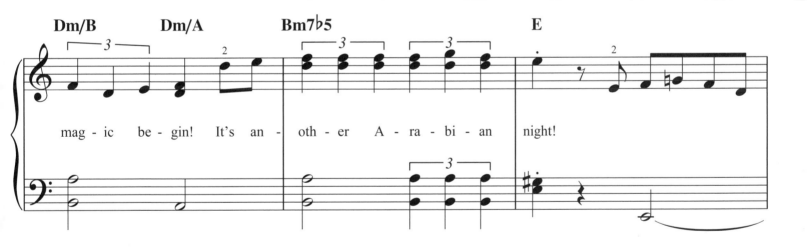

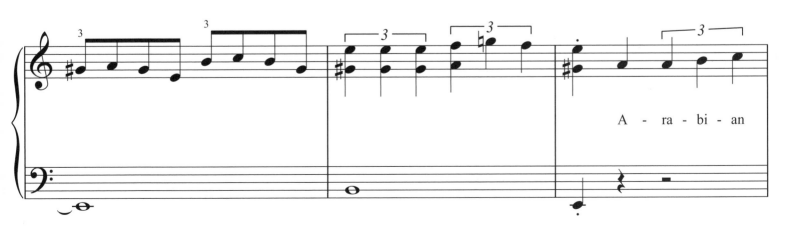

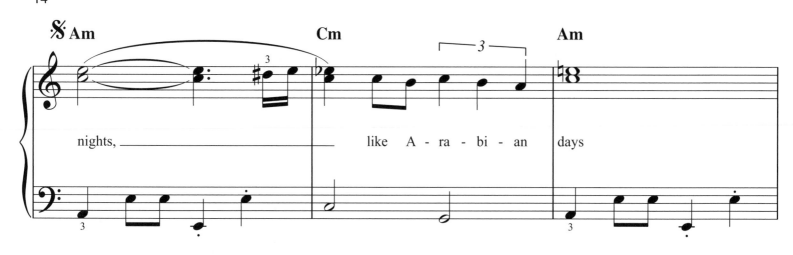

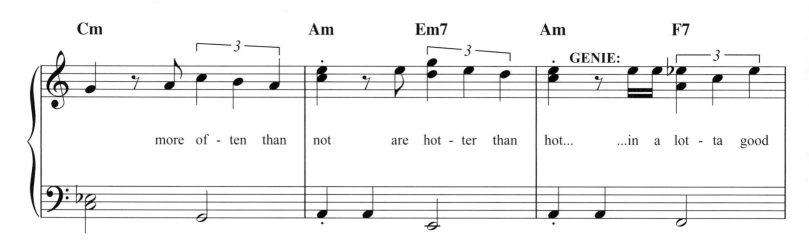

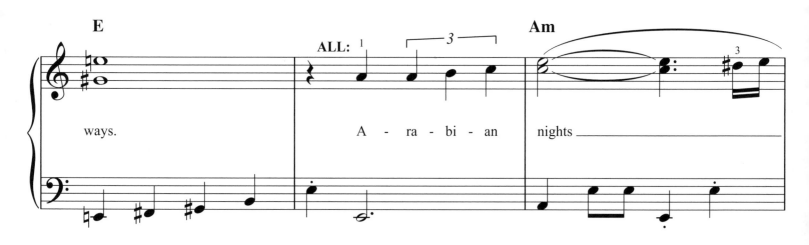

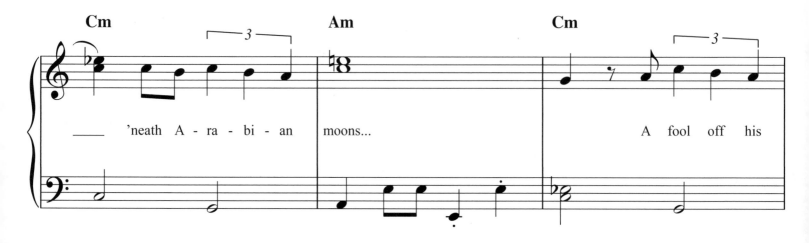

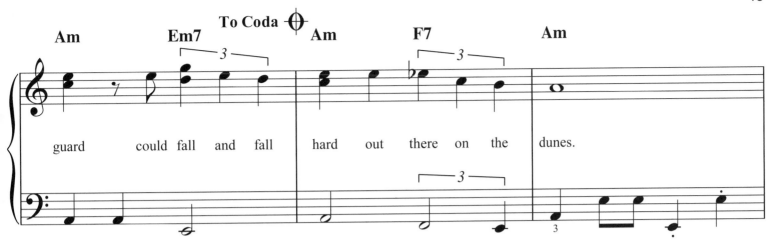

guard could fall and fall hard out there on the dunes.

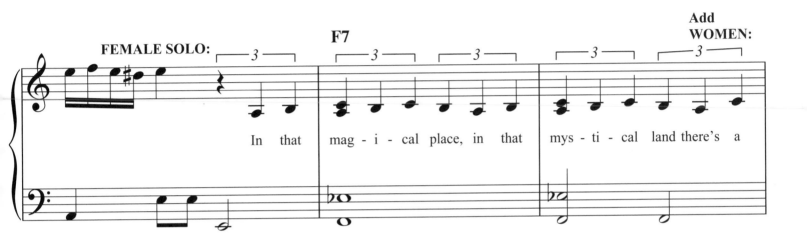

FEMALE SOLO:

In that mag - i - cal place, in that mys - ti - cal land there's a

Add WOMEN:

ge - nie in - side ev - 'ry jar. He'll do all of your bid - ding. Your

MEN:

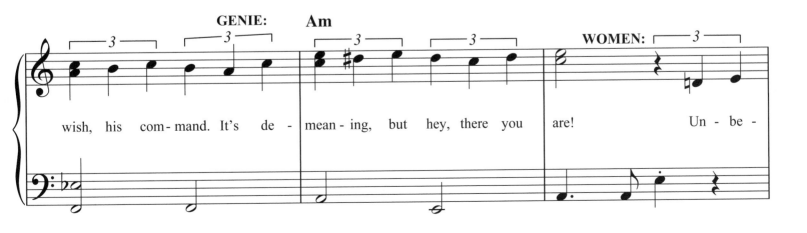

GENIE:

wish, his com - mand. It's de - mean - ing, but hey, there you are! Un - be -

WOMEN:

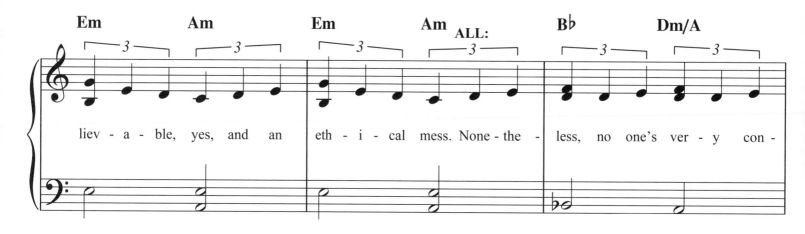

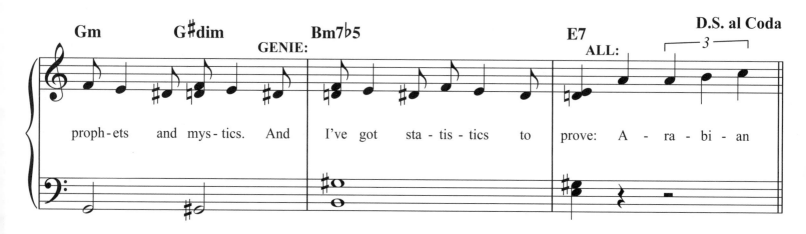

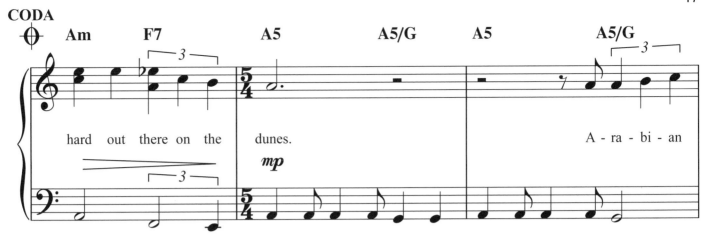

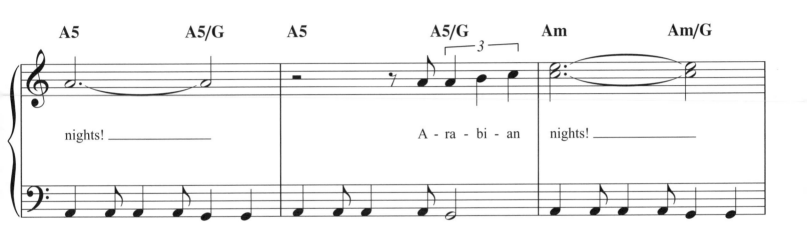

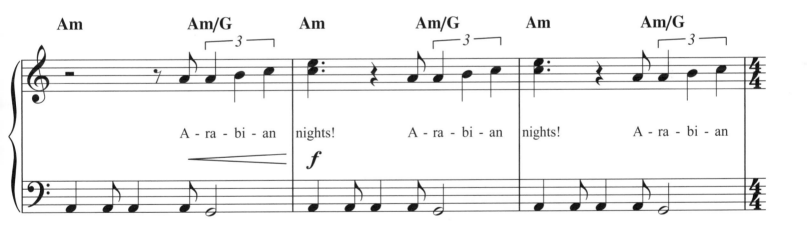

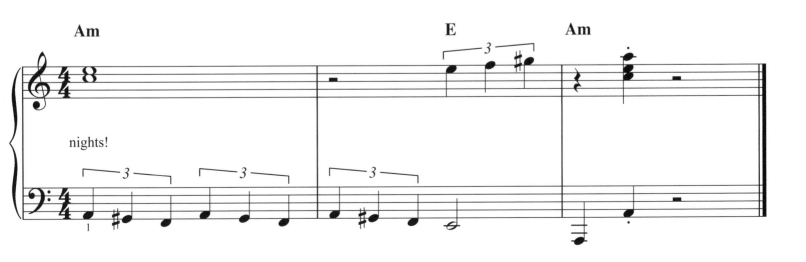

ONE JUMP AHEAD

Music by ALAN MENKEN
Lyrics by TIM RICE

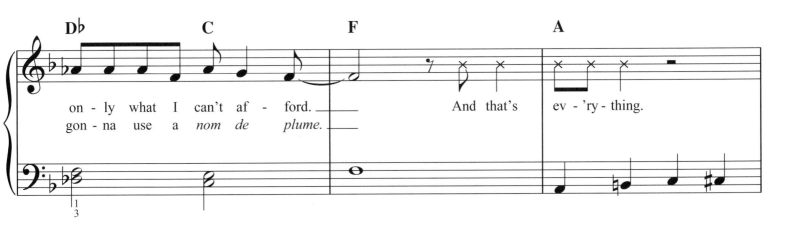

only what I can't af - ford. ___ And that's ev - 'ry - thing.
gon - na use a *nom de plume.* ___

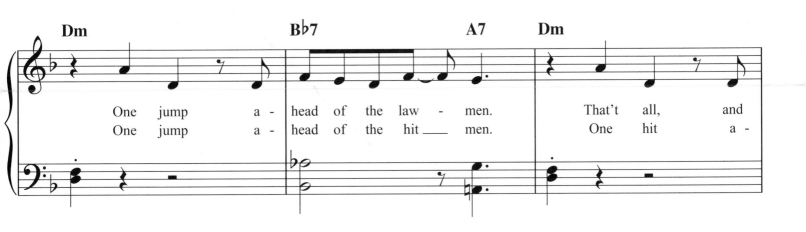

One jump a - head of the law - men. That't all, and
One jump a - head of the hit ___ men. One hit a -

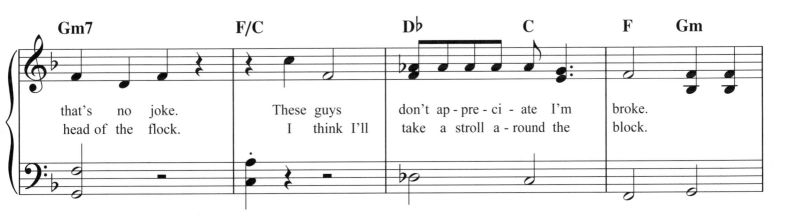

that's no joke. These guys don't ap - pre - ci - ate I'm broke.
head of the flock. I think I'll take a stroll a - round the block.

ENSEMBLE:
Riff raff! ___ Street rat! ___ Scoun - drel! ___
Stop, thief! ___ Van - dal! ___ Out - rage! ___

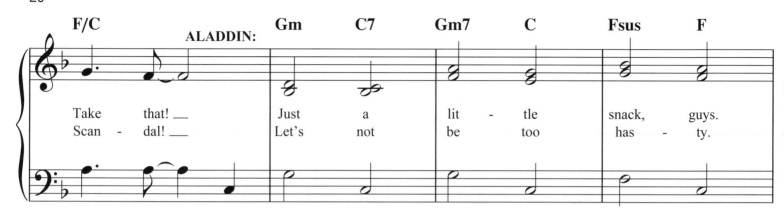

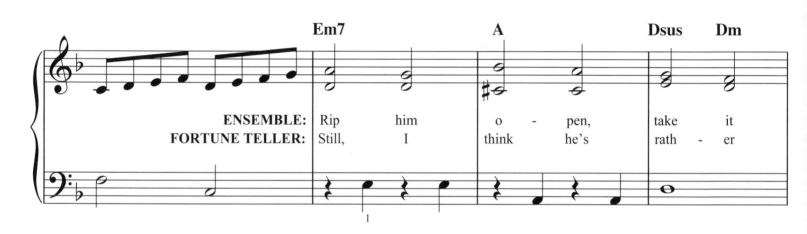

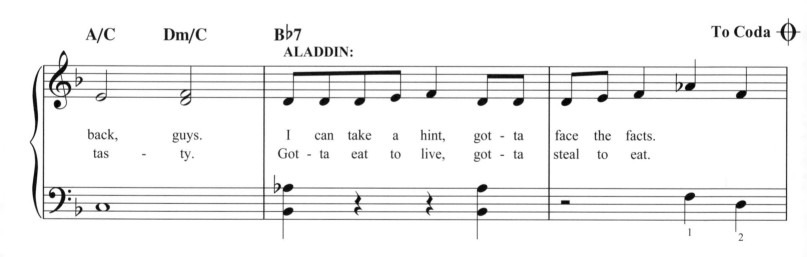

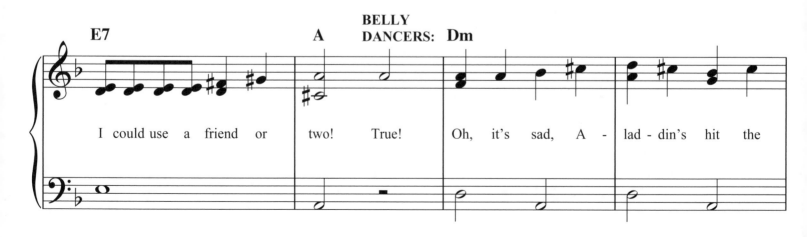

bot - tom.　　　He's be - come a　one - man rise in

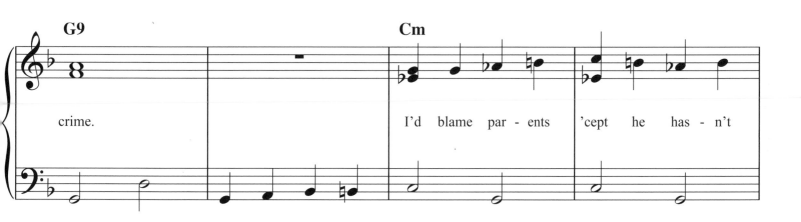

crime.　　　I'd blame par - ents　'cept he has - n't

ALADDIN:

got　'em.　　　Got - ta eat to live, got - ta

D.S. al Coda

steal to eat. Tell you all a - bout it when I got the　time.

CODA

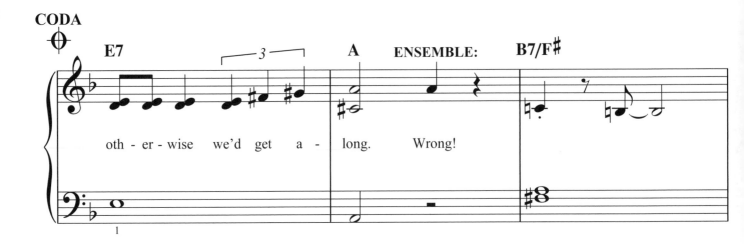

oth - er - wise we'd get a - long. Wrong!

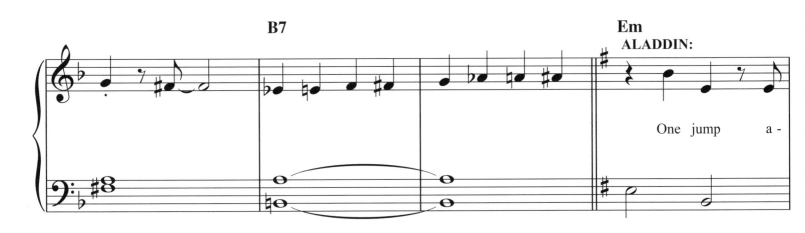

One jump a -

head of the hoof - beats. One hop a - head of the hump. __

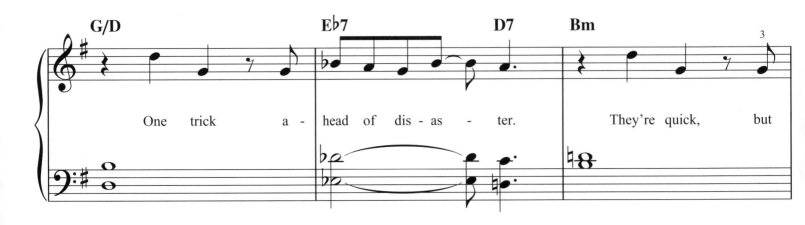

One trick a - head of dis - as - ter. They're quick, but

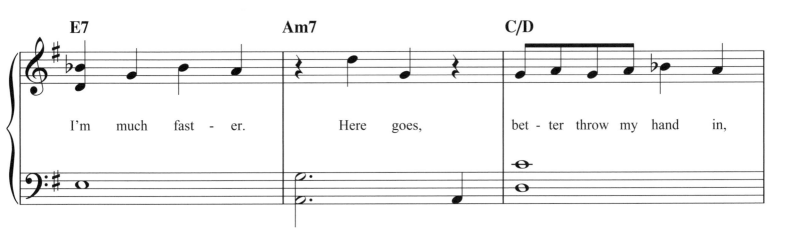

I'm much fast - er. Here goes, bet - ter throw my hand in,

wish me hap - py land - in'. All I got - ta do is jump.

PROUD OF YOUR BOY

Music by ALAN MENKEN
Lyrics by HOWARD ASHMAN

With determination

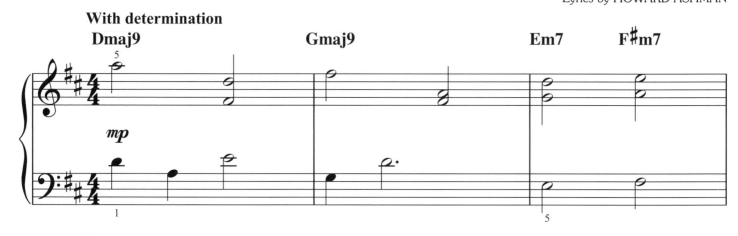

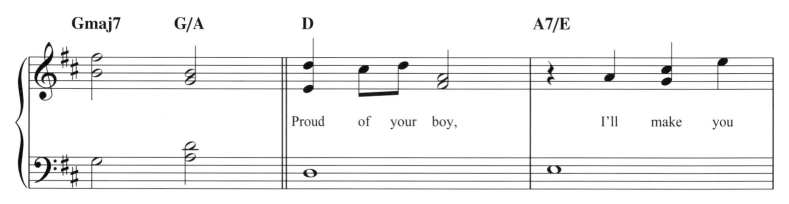

Proud of your boy, I'll make you

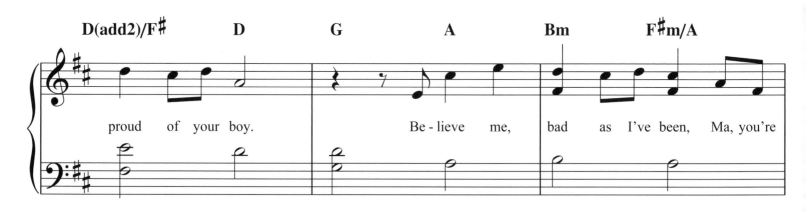

proud of your boy. Be-lieve me, bad as I've been, Ma, you're

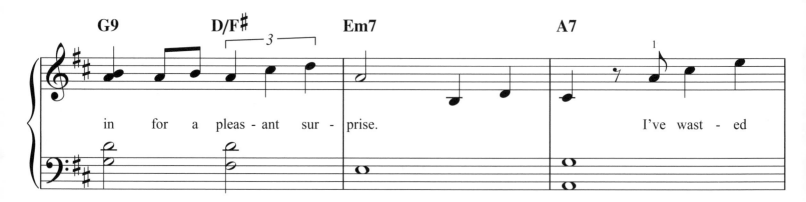

in for a pleas-ant sur-prise. I've wast-ed

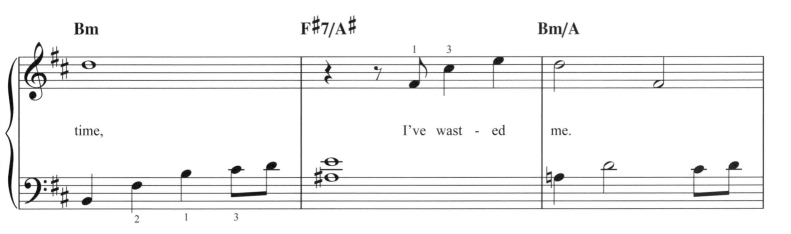

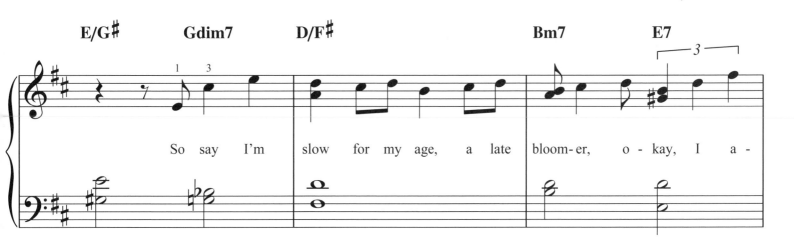

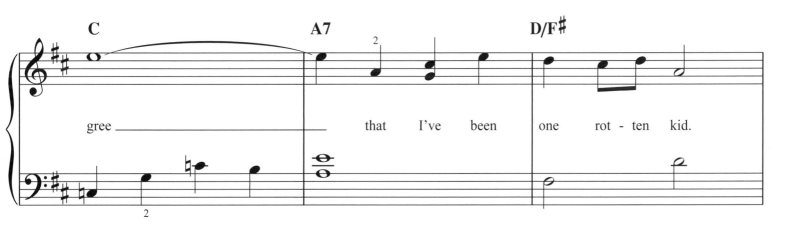

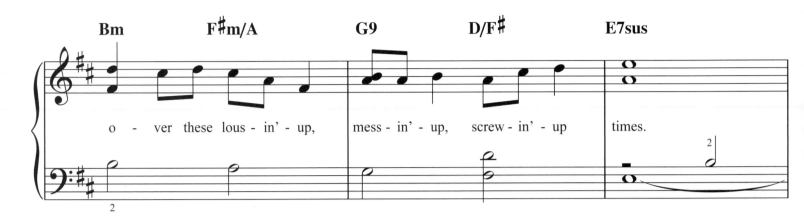

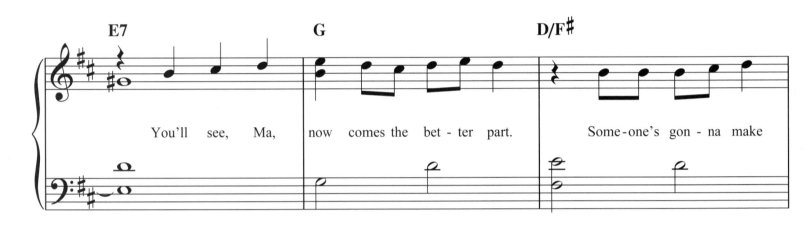

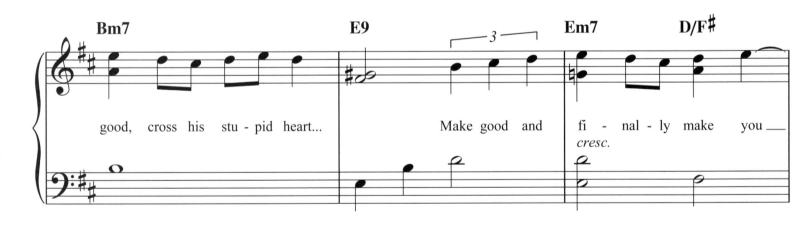

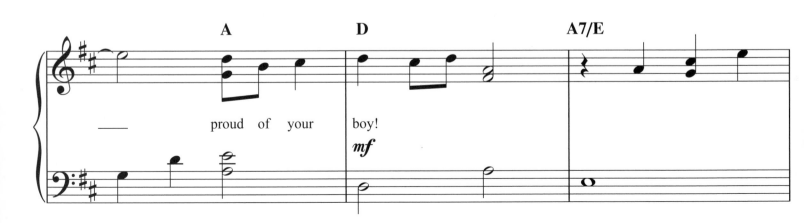

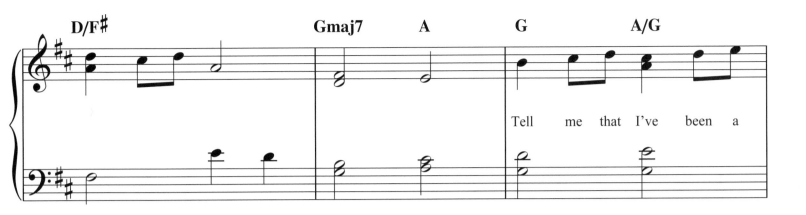

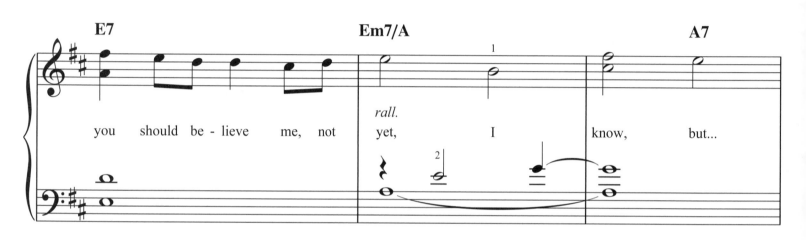

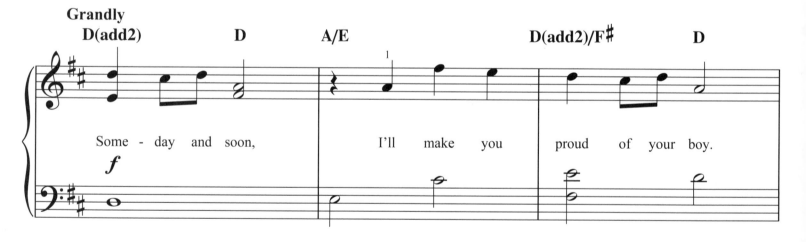

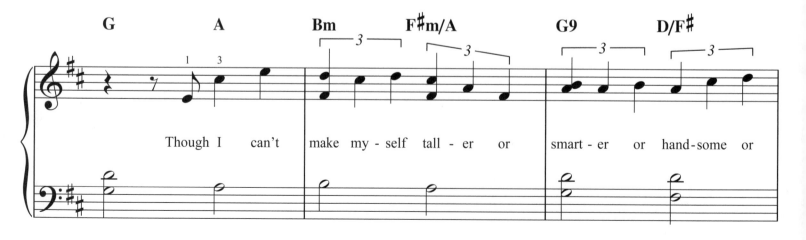

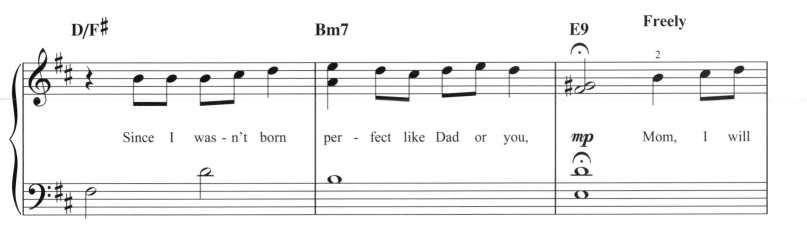

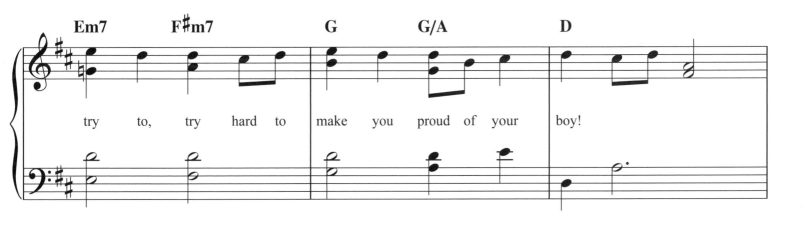

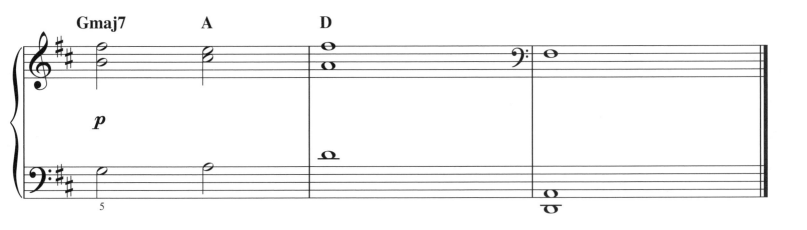

BABKAK, OMAR, ALADDIN, KASSIM

Music by ALAN MENKEN
Lyrics by HOWARD ASHMAN

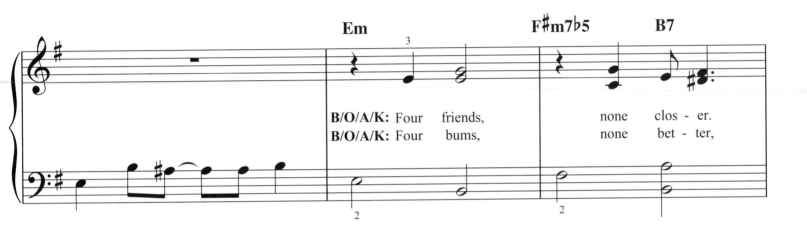

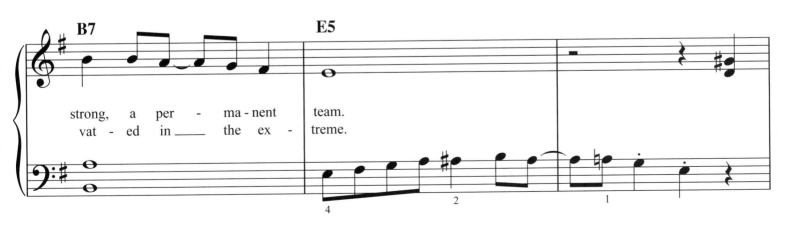

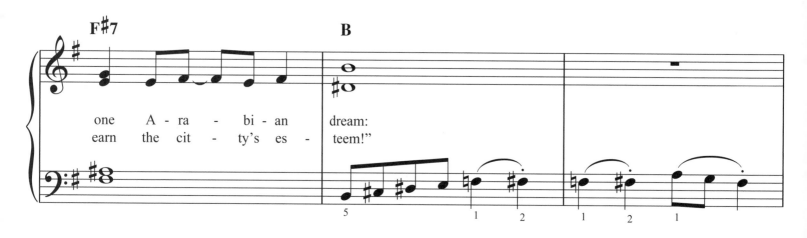

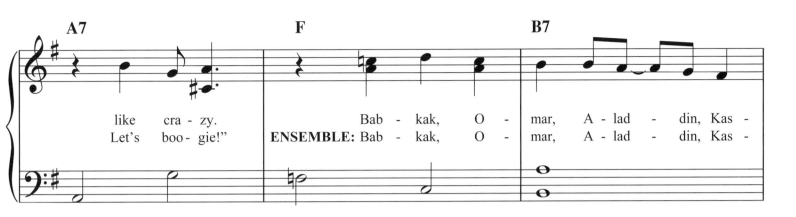

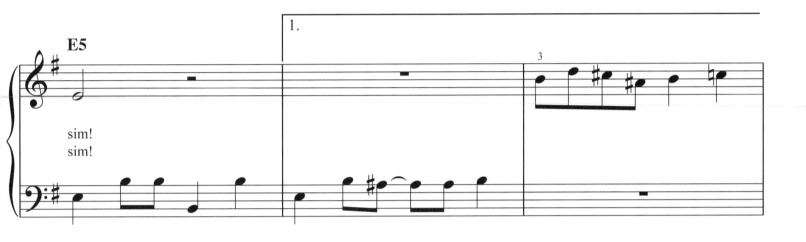

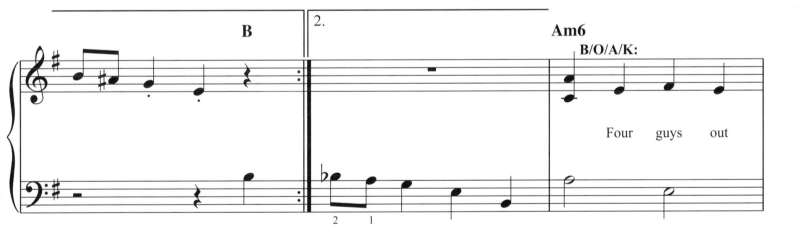

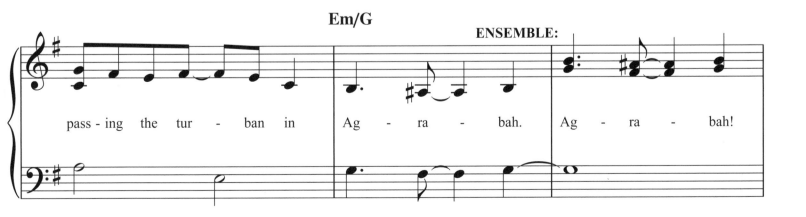

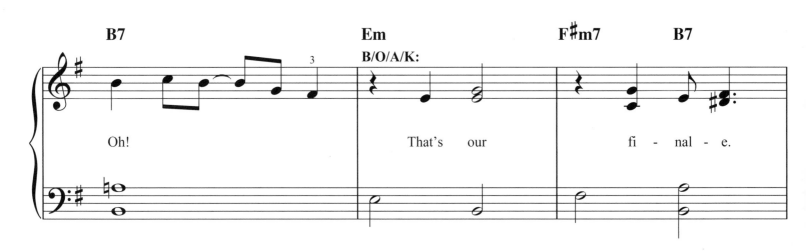

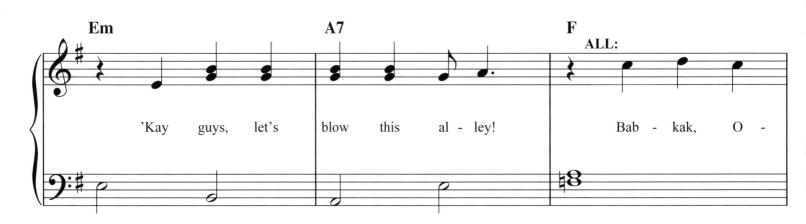

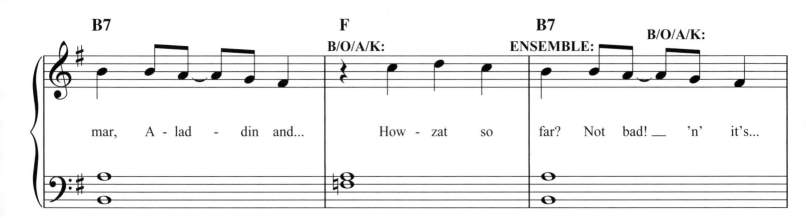

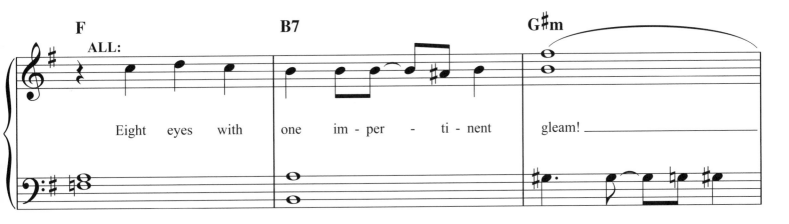

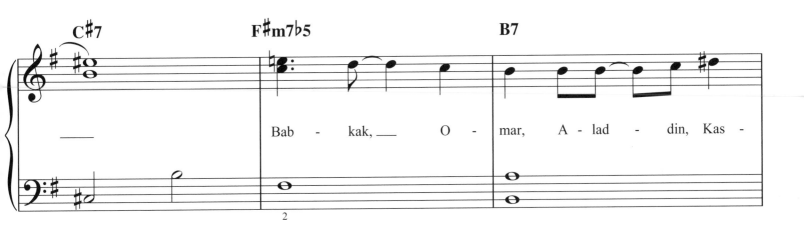

A MILLION MILES AWAY

Music by ALAN MENKEN
Lyrics by CHAD BEGUELIN

Romantic Rock Ballad

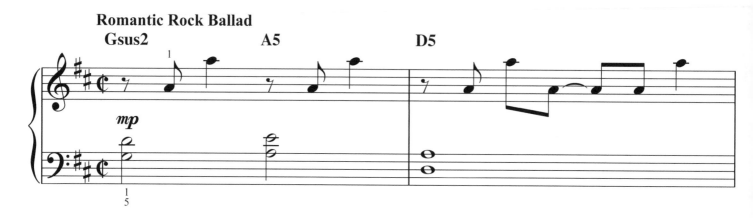

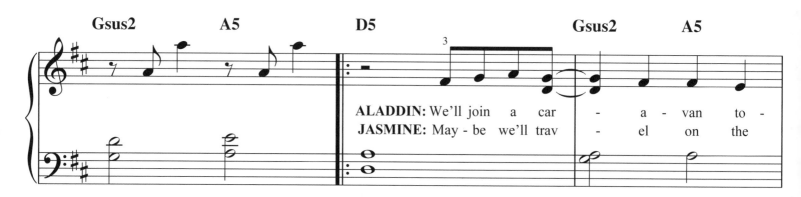

ALADDIN: We'll join a car - a - van to -
JASMINE: May - be we'll trav - el on the

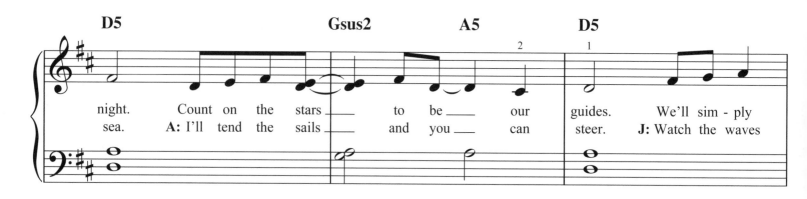

night. Count on the stars ___ to be ___ our guides. We'll sim - ply
sea. **A:** I'll tend the sails ___ and you ___ can steer. **J:** Watch the waves

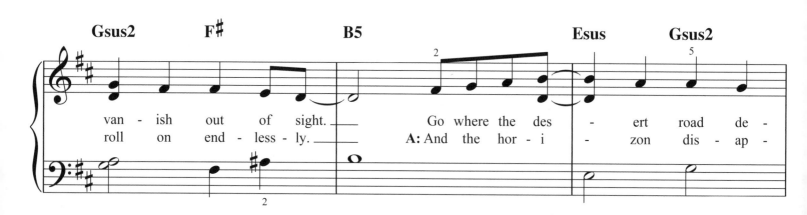

van - ish out of sight. ___ Go where the des - ert road de -
roll on end - less - ly. ___ **A:** And the hor - i - zon dis - ap -

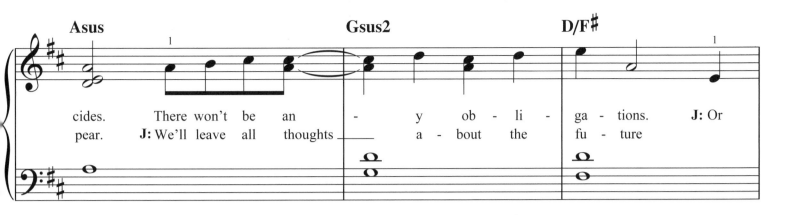

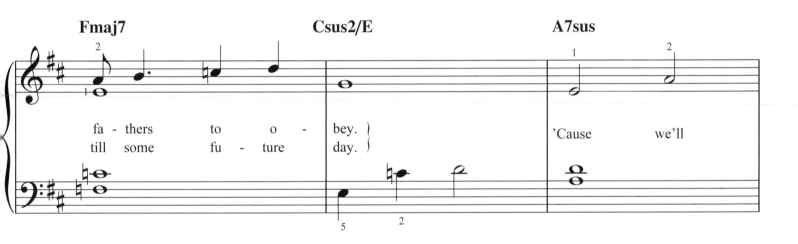

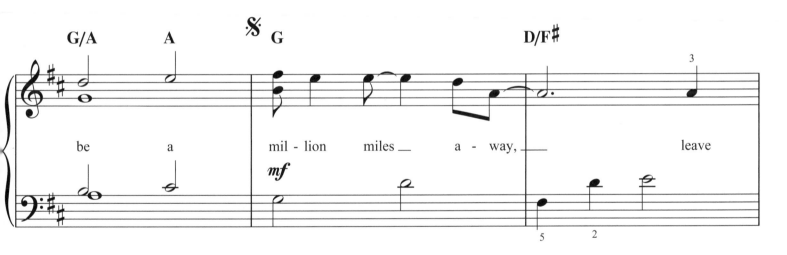

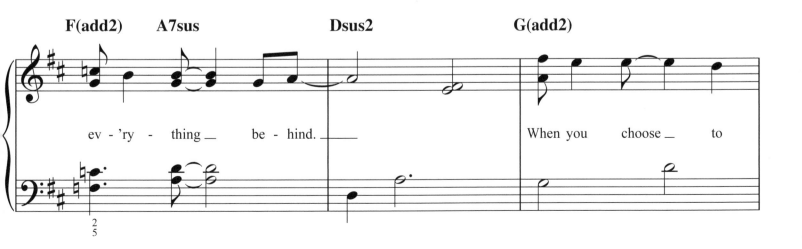

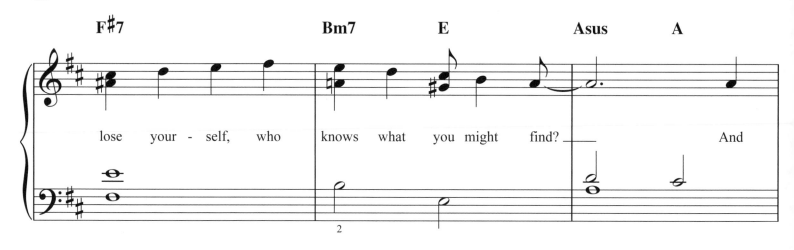

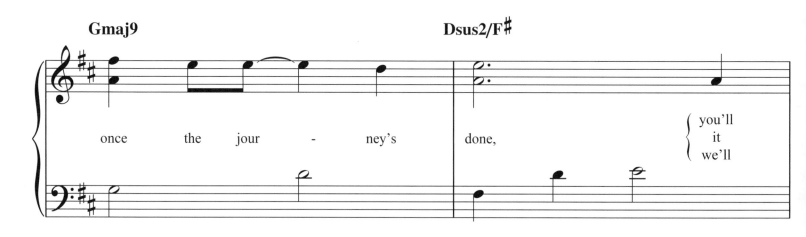

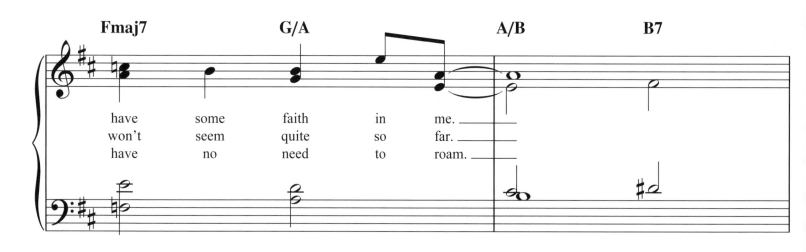

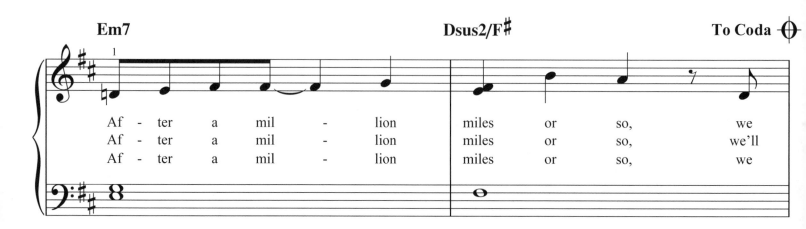

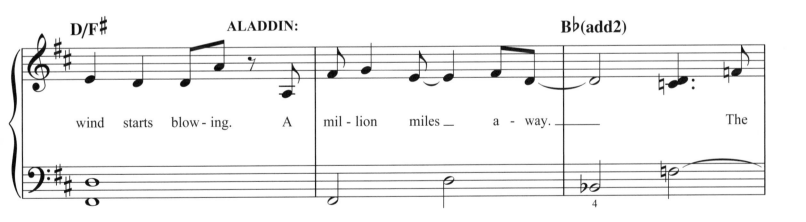

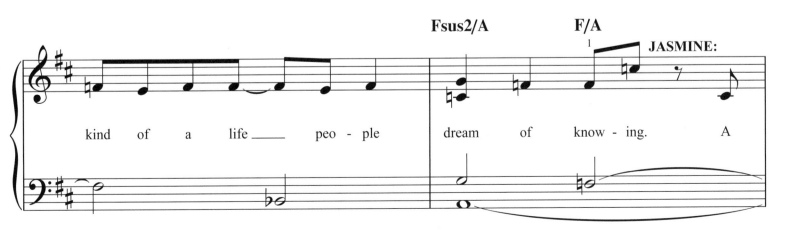

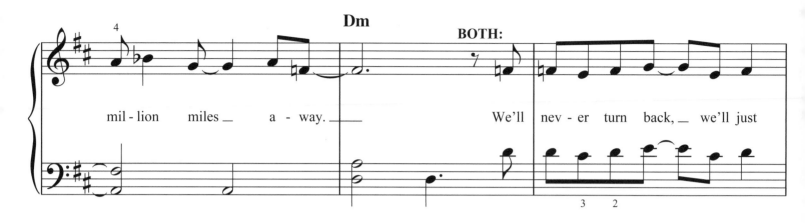

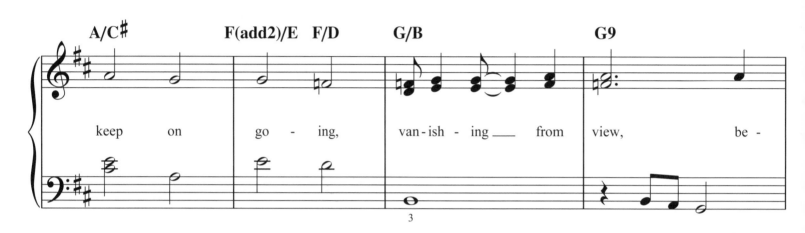

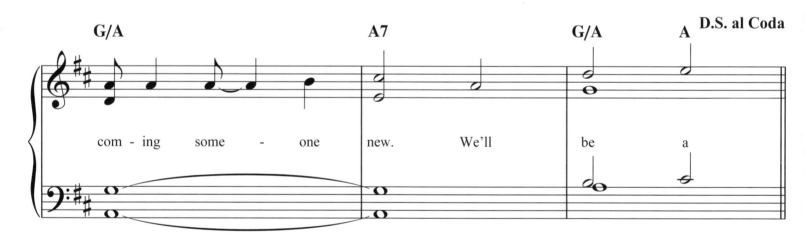

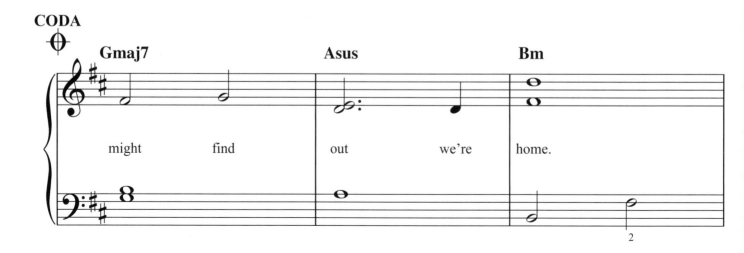

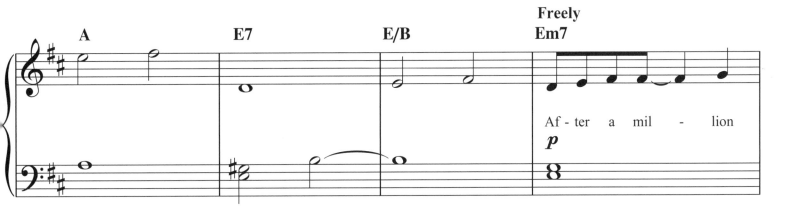

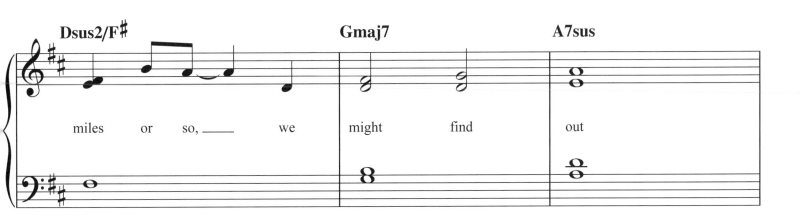

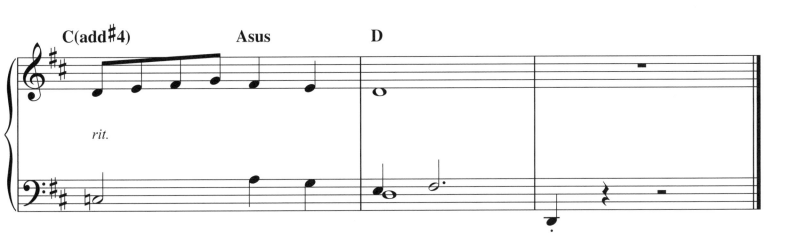

FRIEND LIKE ME

Music by ALAN MENKEN
Lyrics by HOWARD ASHMAN

Rollicking Swing

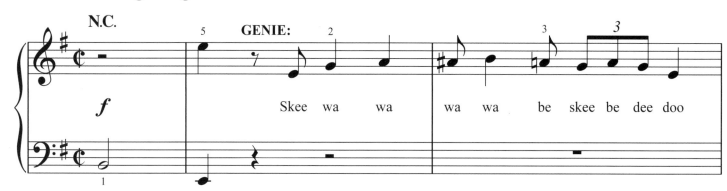

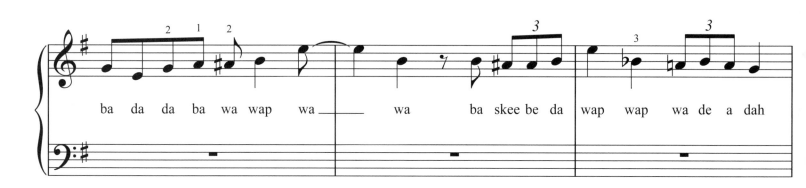

ba - ba had them / pow - er in your

for - ty thieves, She - her - a - / cor - ner now, some heav - y

za - da had a thou-sand tales. / am - mu - ni - tion in your camp.

But, Mas - ter, you're in luck, 'cause / You got some punch pi - zazz, ya -

up your sleeves _ you got a / hoo, and how! _ See all you

brand of ma - gic nev - er / got - ta do is rub that

1.

fails. You got some

2.

lamp, and I'll _ say:

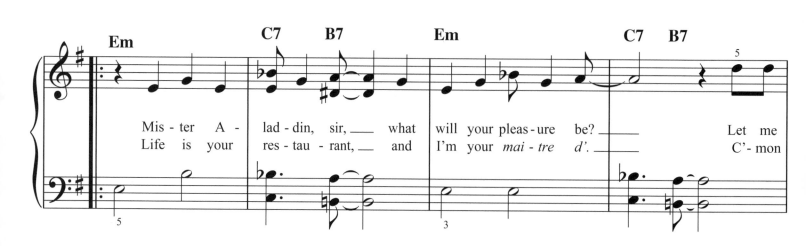

Mis - ter A - / Life is your

lad - din, sir, _ what / res - tau - rant, _ and

will your pleas - ure be? _ / I'm your *mai - tre d'*. _

Let me / C' - mon

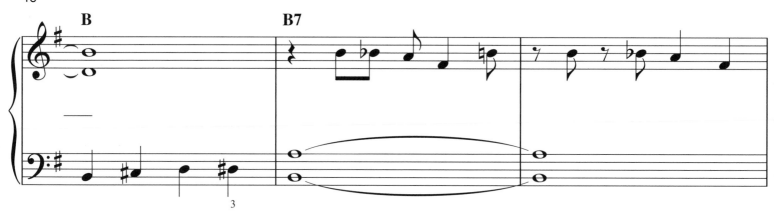

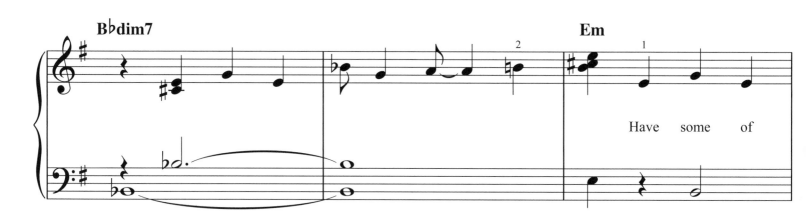

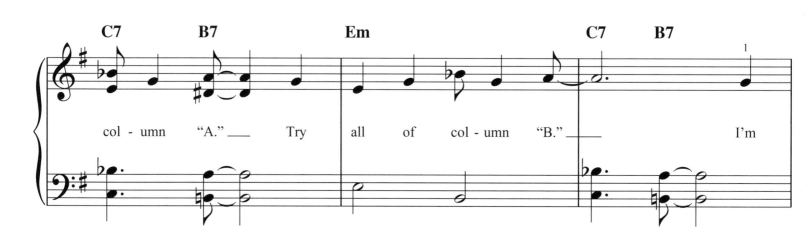

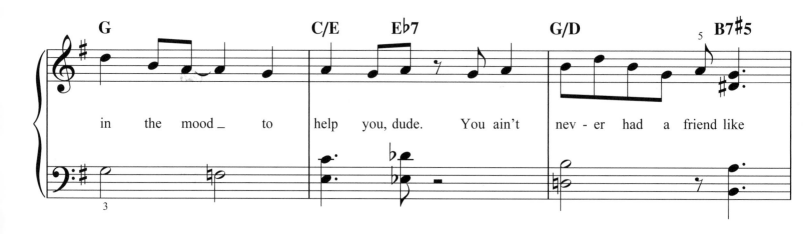

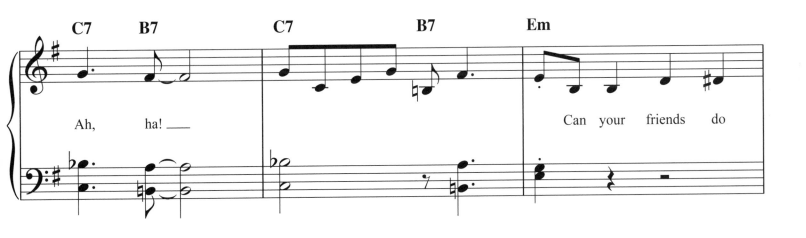

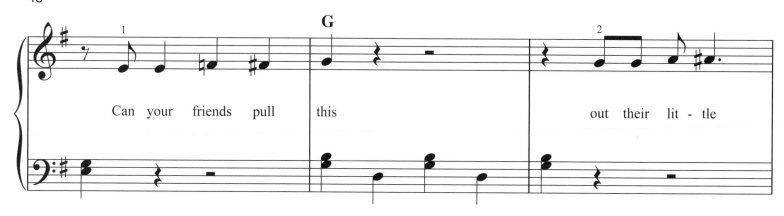

Can your friends pull this   out their lit - tle

hat?   Can your friends go   poof!

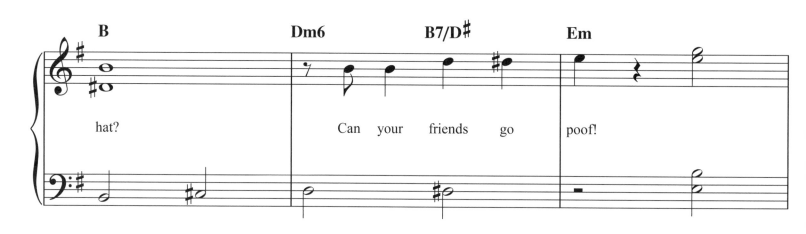

Well, look - y   here!   Can your friends go

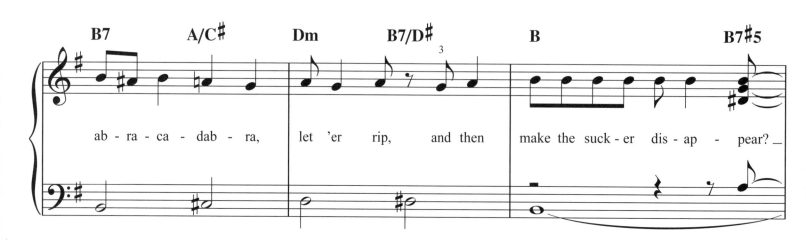

ab - ra - ca - dab - ra,   let 'er rip, and then   make the suck - er dis - ap - pear? _

So don-'cha sit there slack - jawed, bug - gy eyed. I'm here to
help you out. So what - cha

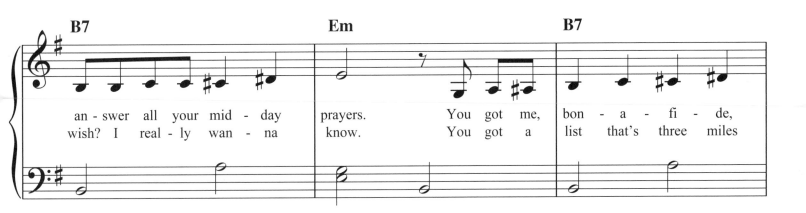

an - swer all your mid - day prayers. You got me, bon - a - fi - de,
wish? I real - ly wan - na know. You got a list that's three miles

cer - ti - fied. ___ You got a ge - nie for your *charge d'af -* *faires.* I got a
long, no doubt. ___ Well, all you got - ta do is rub like

pow - er - ful urge to so...

Slower Strut

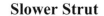

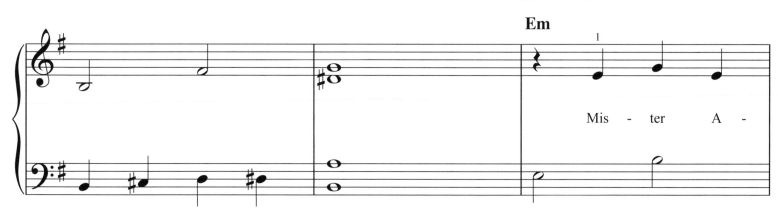

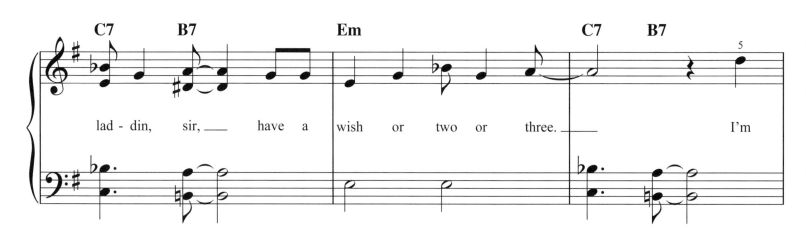

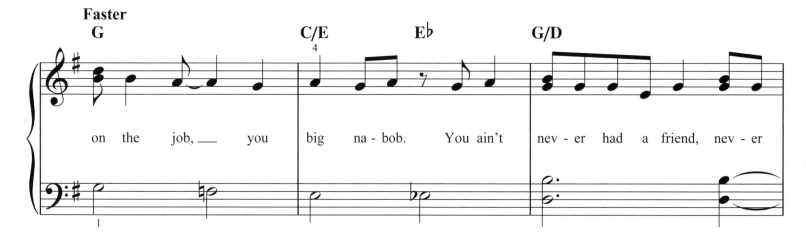

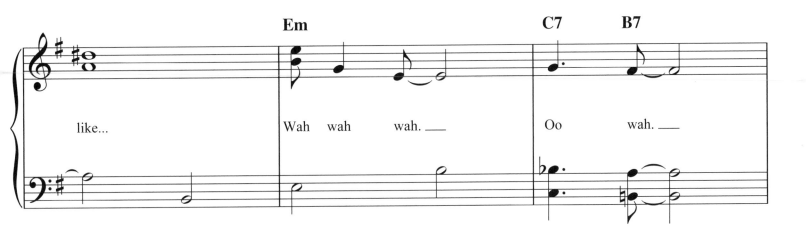

PRINCE ALI

Music by ALAN MENKEN
Lyrics by HOWARD ASHMAN

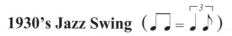

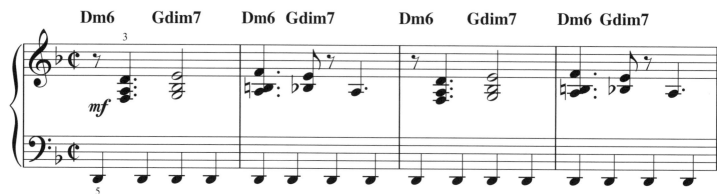

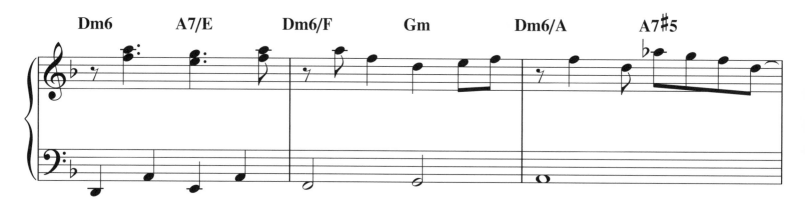

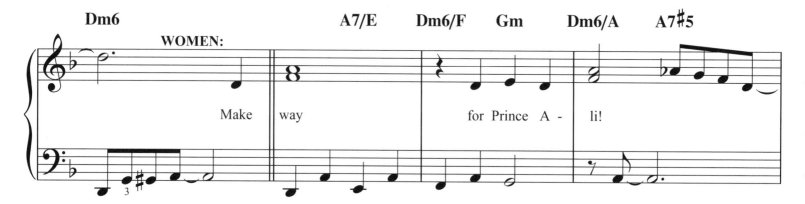

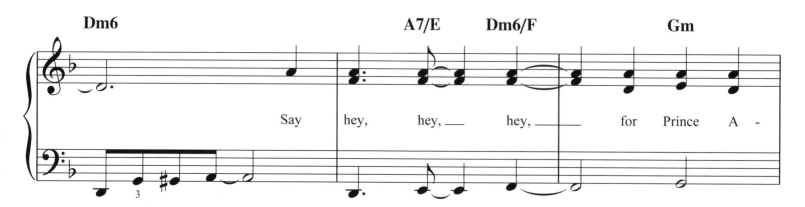

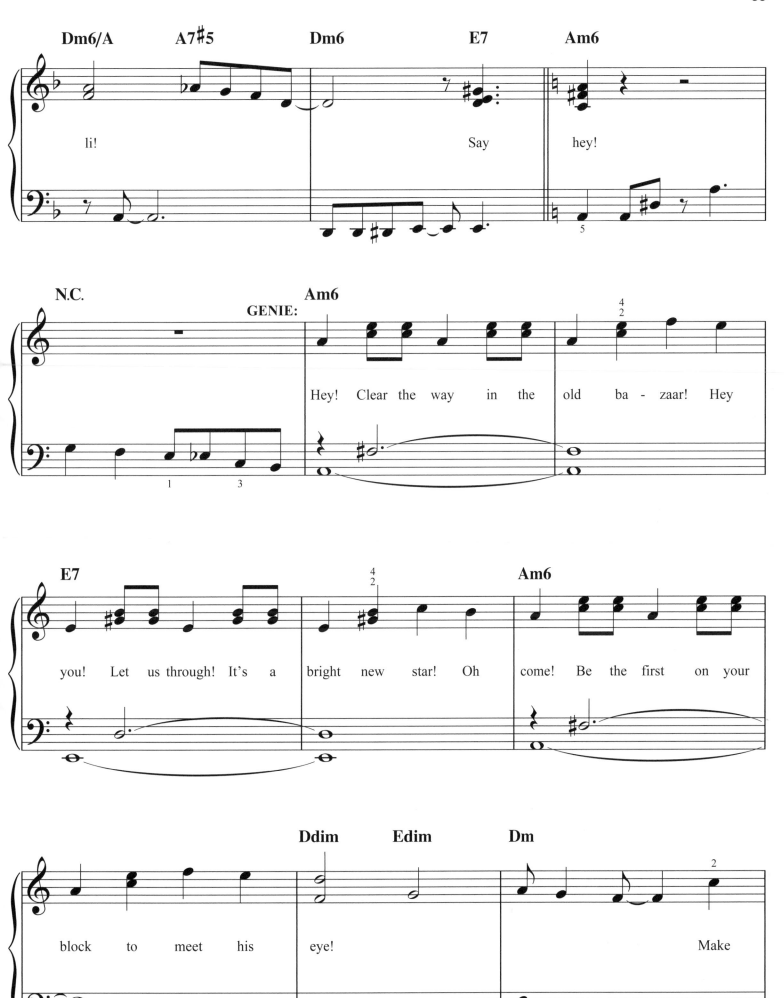

B7 ... way! Here he comes! Ring bells! Bang the drums! Are **E** you gon-na love this

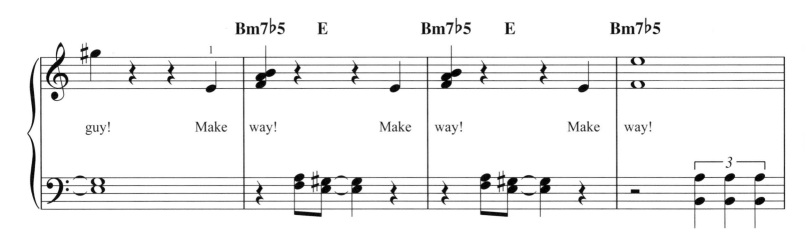

Bm7♭5 **E** **Bm7♭5** **E** **Bm7♭5**
guy! Make way! Make way! Make way!

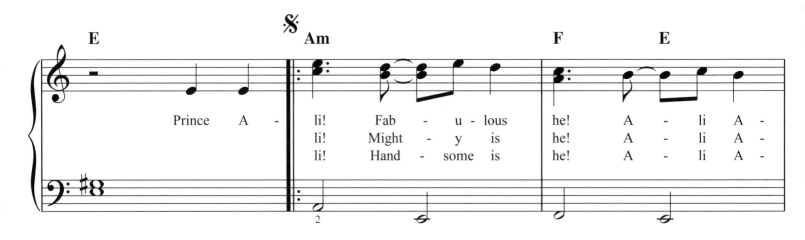

E Prince A - **Am** li! Fab - u - lous **F** he! A - **E** li A -
li! Might - y is he! A - li A -
li! Hand - some is he! A - li A -

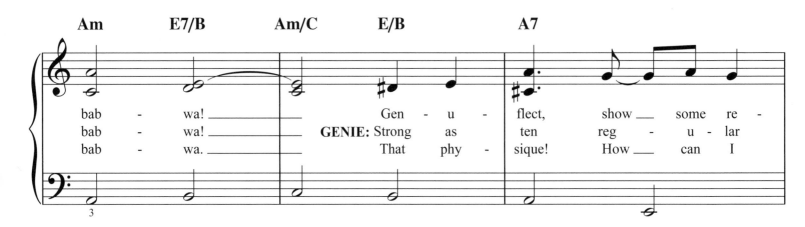

Am bab - wa! **E7/B** **Am/C** **E/B** Gen - u - **A7** flect, show __ some re -
bab - wa! **GENIE:** Strong as ten reg - u - lar
bab - wa. That phy - sique! How __ can I

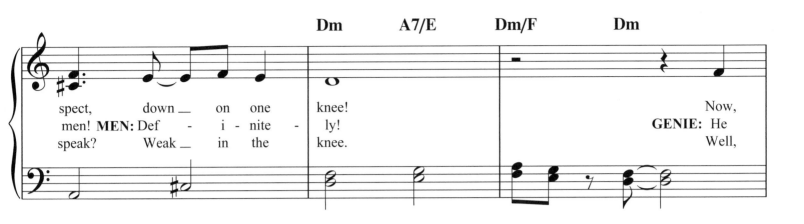

Dm   **A7/E**   **Dm/F**   **Dm**

spect,   down __ on one | knee! | | Now,
men! **MEN:** Def - i - nite - | ly! | **GENIE:** He
speak?   Weak __ in the | knee. | | Well,

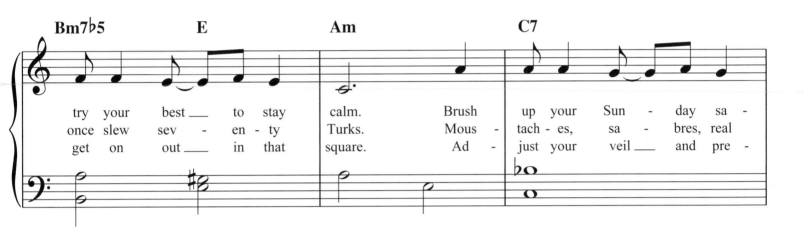

Bm7♭5   **E**   **Am**   **C7**

try your best __ to stay | calm.   Brush | up your Sun - day sa -
once slew sev - en - ty | Turks.   Mous - | tach - es, sa - bres, real
get on out __ in that | square.   Ad - | just your veil __ and pre -

F   **1.** **B7**   **2.**

laam.   Then | come and meet __ his spec - | tac - u - lar co - ter -
jerks!   Who |
pare   to |

N.C.   **Add MEN:**   **2.** **B7**

ie. | Prince A - | gave those bad __ guys the
 | | gawk and grov - el and

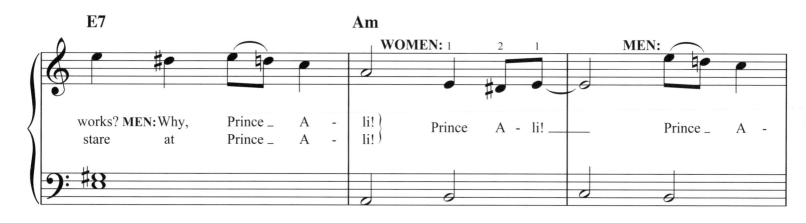

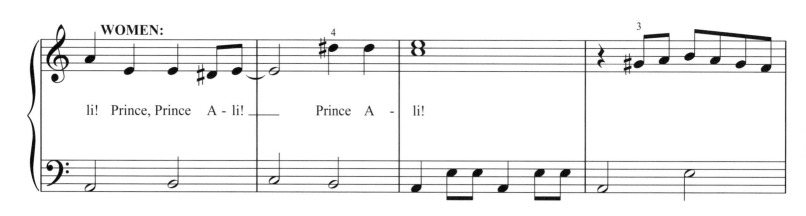

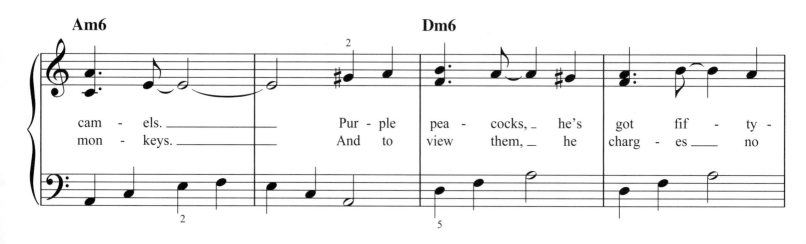

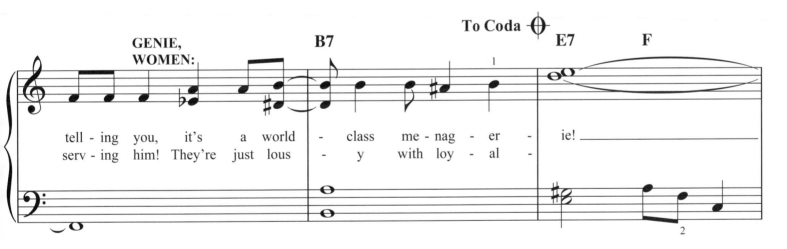

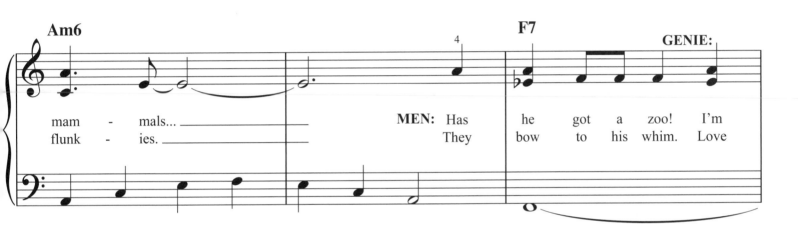

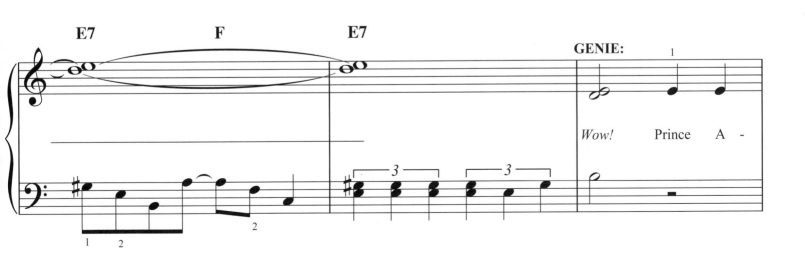

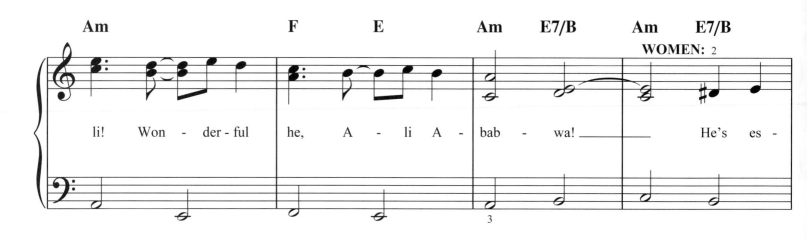

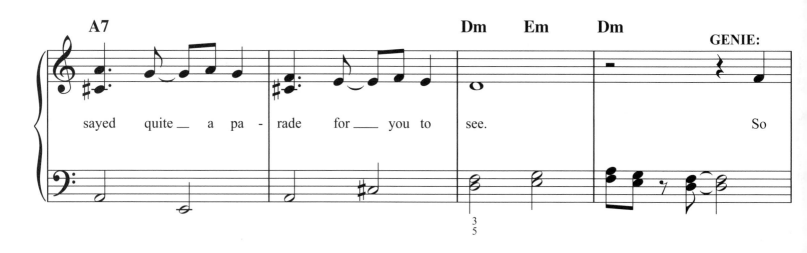

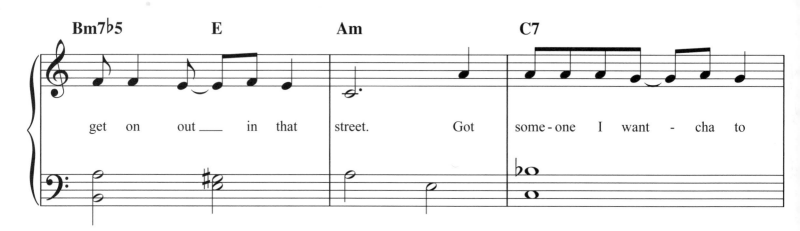

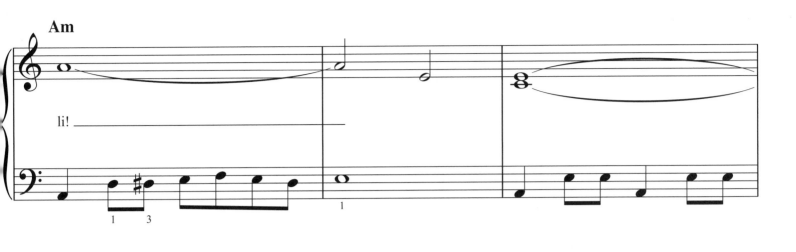

li! _____

MEN: **Am6**

Sing hey, hey! ___ Hey, hey! ___ Sing

straight eighths

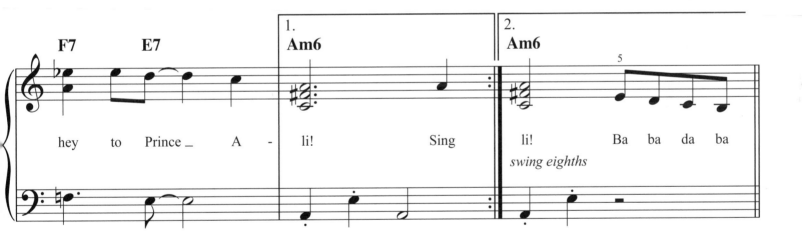

F7 **E7** | **1.** **Am6** | **2.** **Am6**

hey to Prince _ A - li! Sing li! Ba ba da ba

swing eighths

Am **GENIE:**

da. Ba ba da ba da. There's no ques-tion this A -

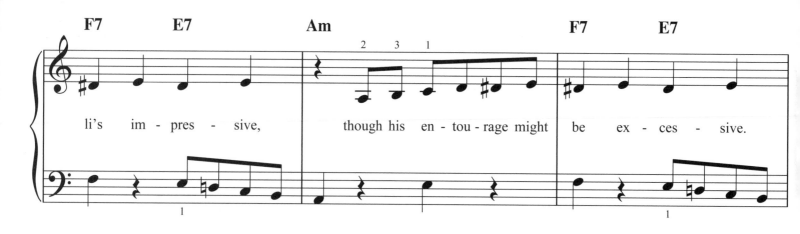

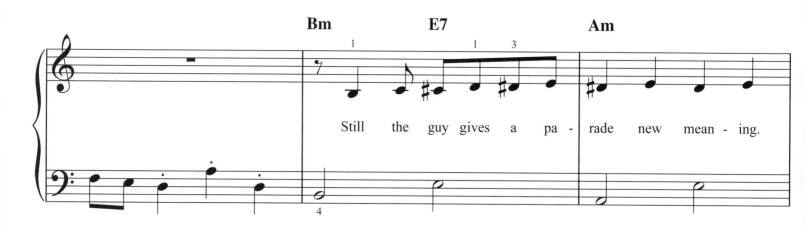

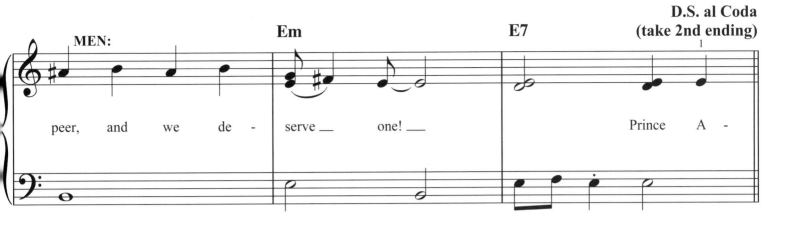

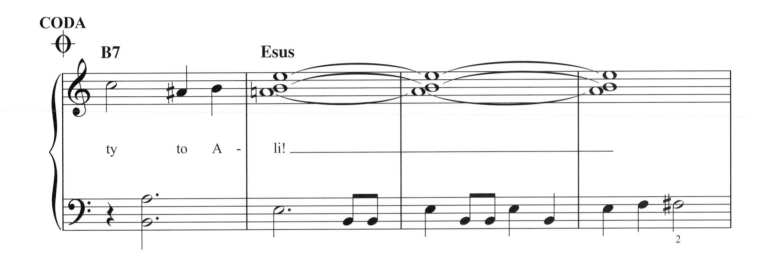

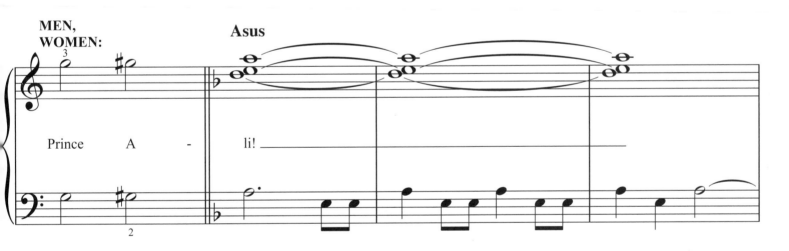

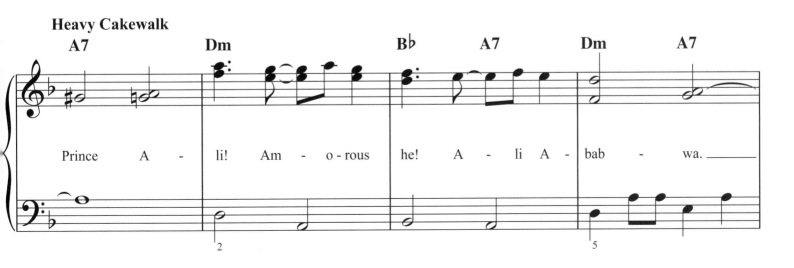

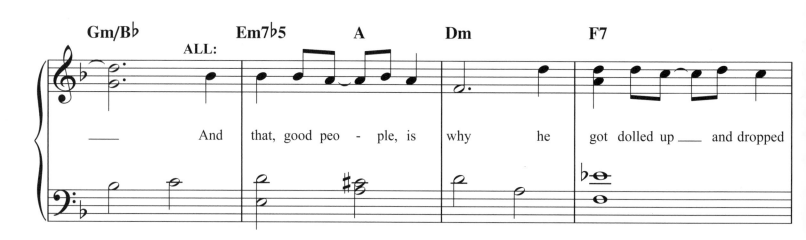

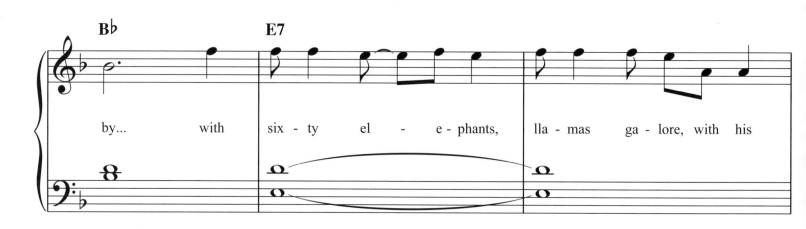

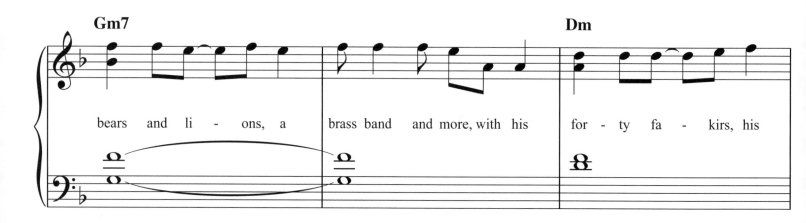

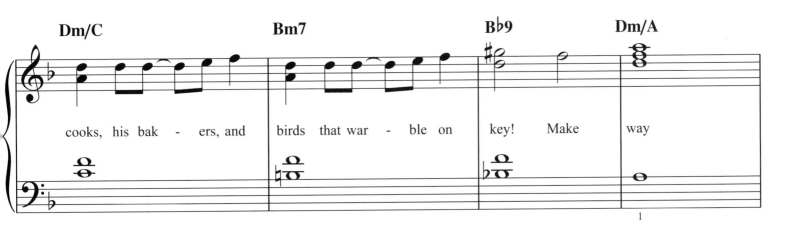

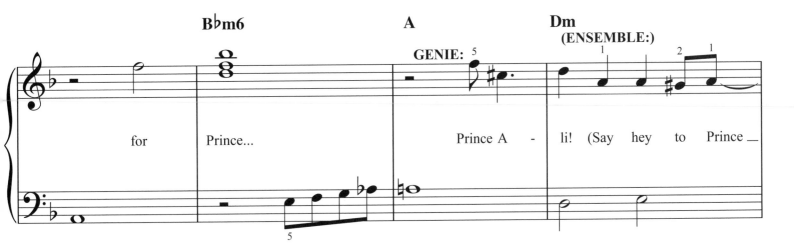

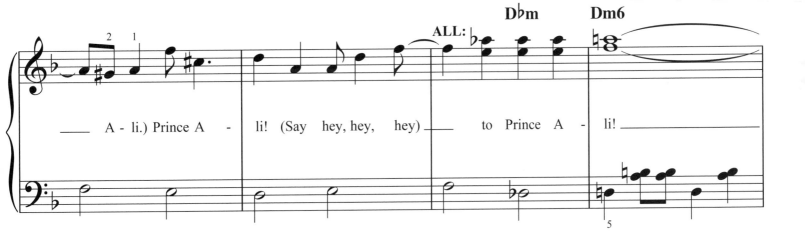

A WHOLE NEW WORLD

Music by ALAN MENKEN
Lyrics by TIM RICE

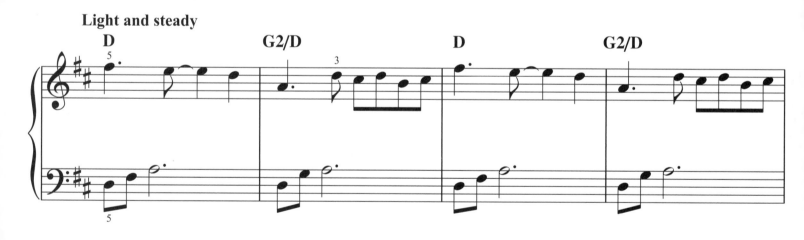

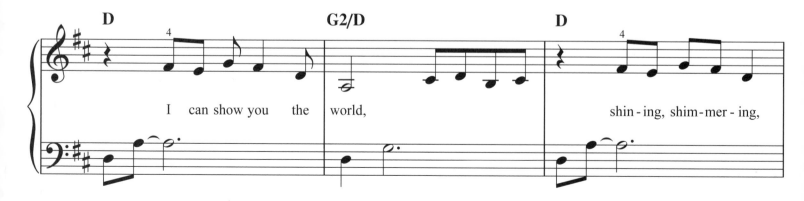

splen - did.   Tell me, Prin - cess, now when did you last

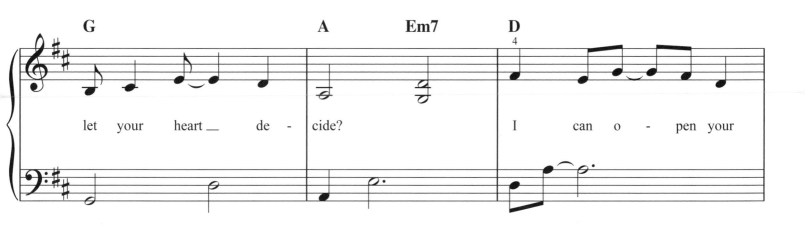

let your heart __ de - cide?   I can o - pen your

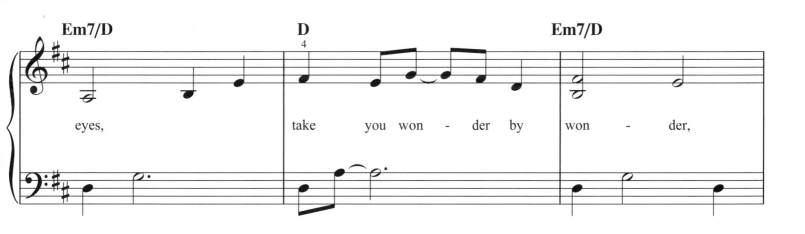

eyes,   take you won - der by won - der,

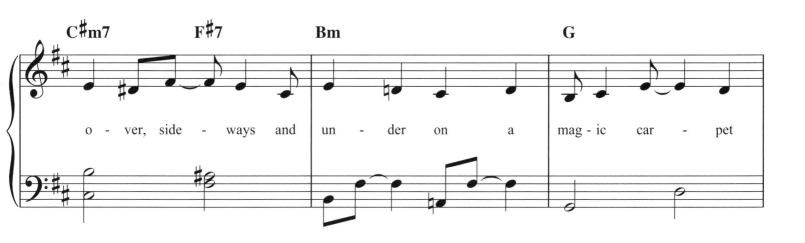

o - ver, side - ways and un - der on a   mag - ic car - pet

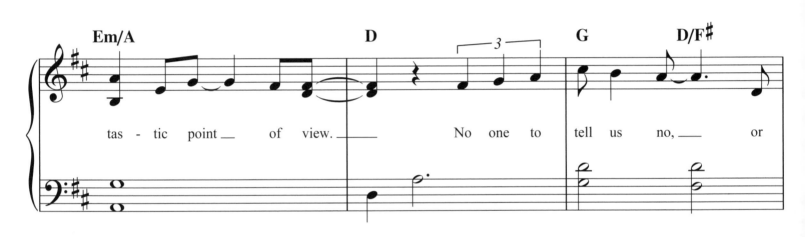

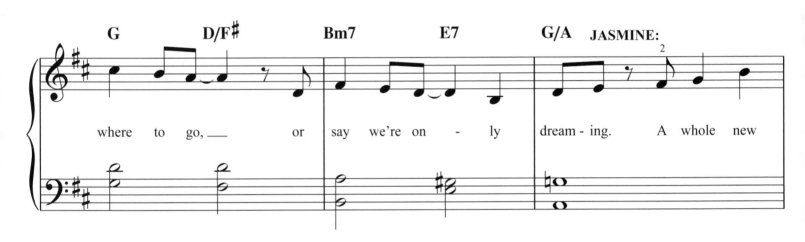

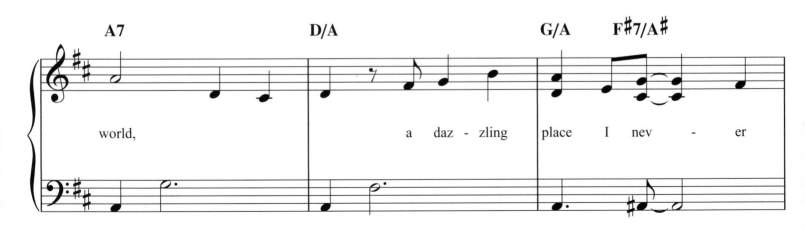

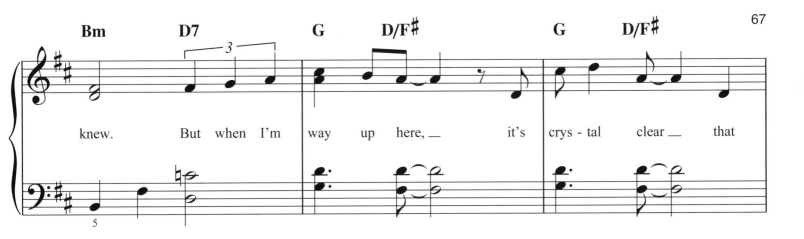

knew. But when I'm way up here, ___ it's crys- tal clear ___ that

now I'm in a whole new world with you.

ALADDIN:
Now I'm in ___ a whole new world with

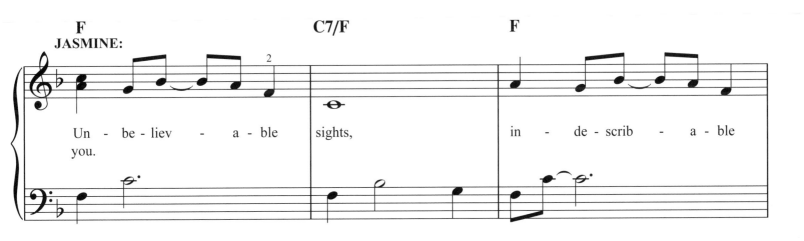

JASMINE:
Un - be- liev - a - ble sights, in - de- scrib - a - ble

you.

feel - ing, soar- ing, tum - bling, free - wheel- ing through an

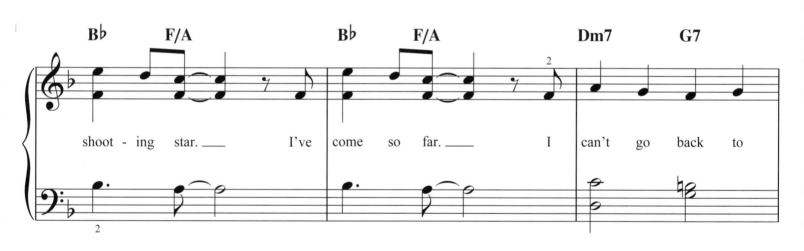

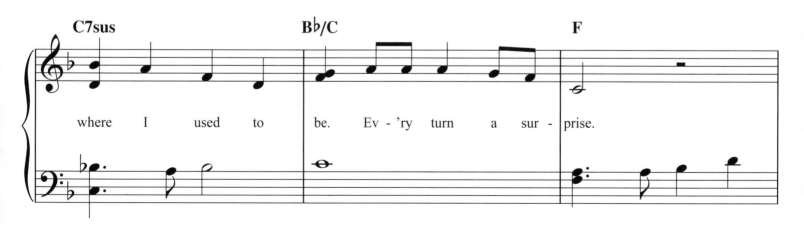

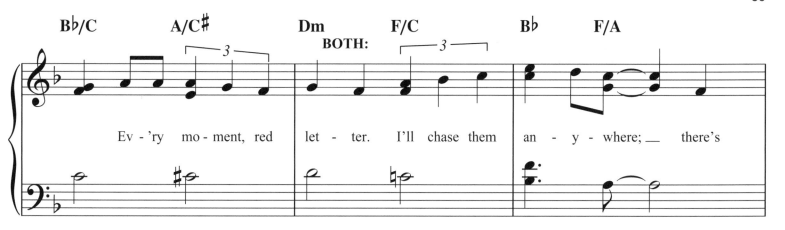

Ev - 'ry mo - ment, red let - ter. I'll chase them an - y - where; ___ there's

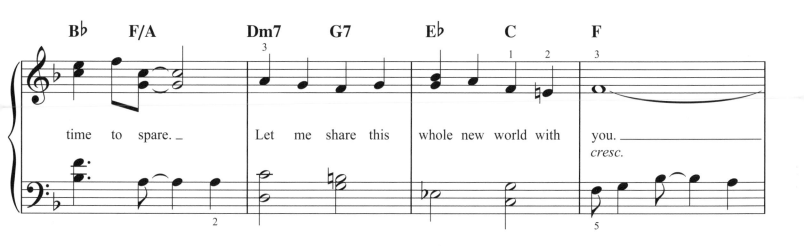

time to spare. ___ Let me share this whole new world with you. ___

cresc.

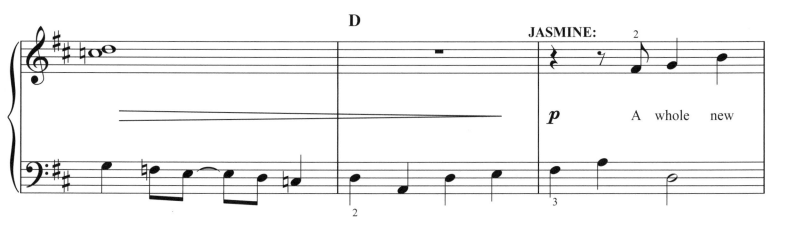

JASMINE:

A whole new

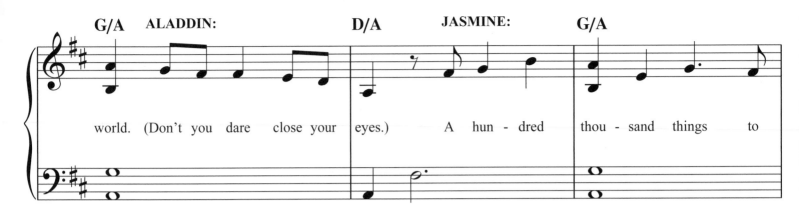

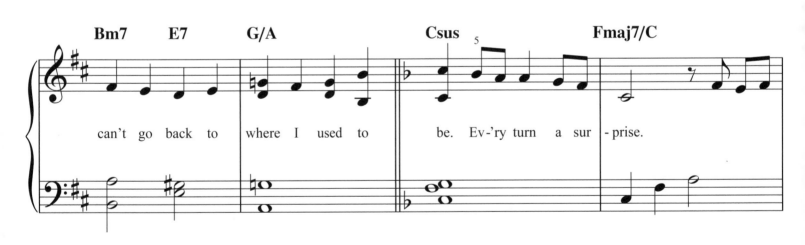

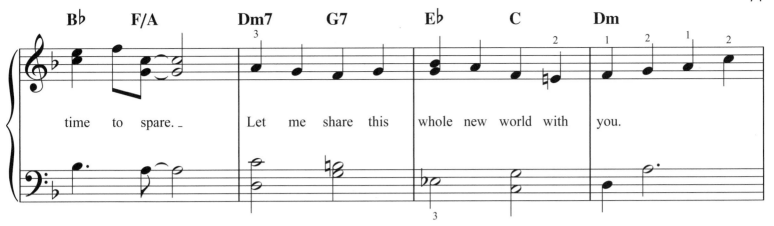

time to spare. Let me share this whole new world with you.

Winding down

A whole new world, (A whole new world,) that's where we'll be. (that's where we'll

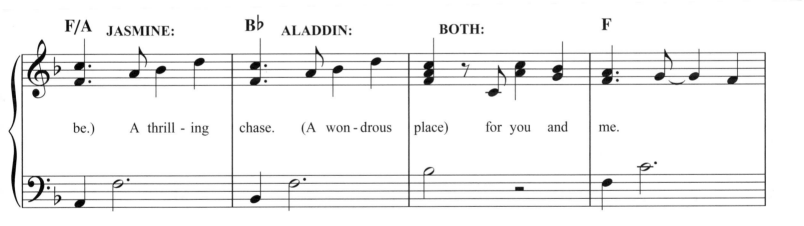

be.) A thrill - ing chase. (A won - drous place) for you and me.

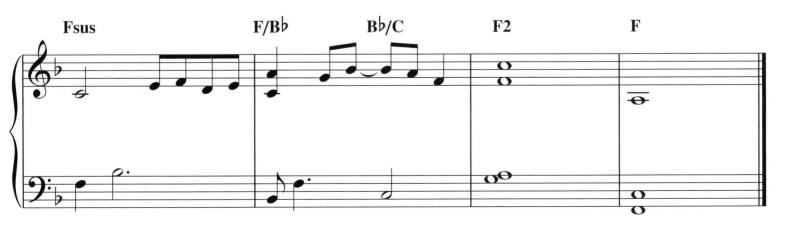

HIGH ADVENTURE

Music by ALAN MENKEN
Lyrics by HOWARD ASHMAN

Brisk Gallop

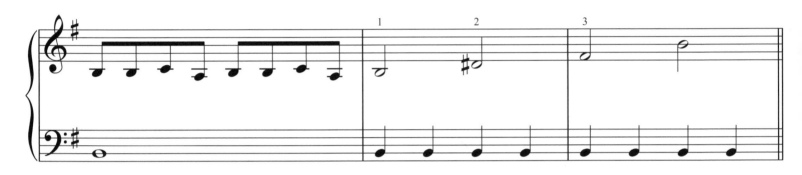

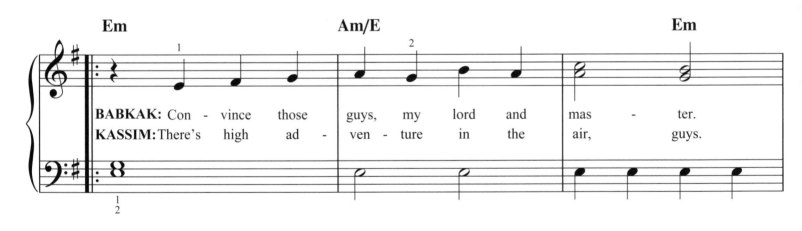

BABKAK: Con - vince those guys, my lord and mas - ter.
KASSIM: There's high ad - ven - ture in the air, guys.

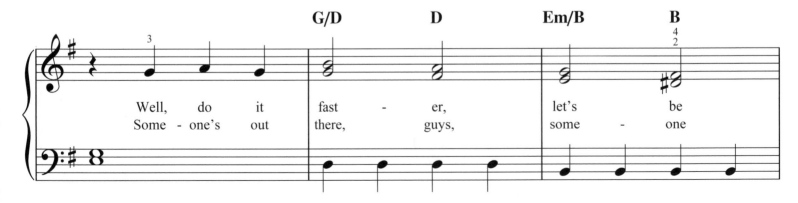

Well, do it fast - er, let's be
Some - one's out there, guys, some - one

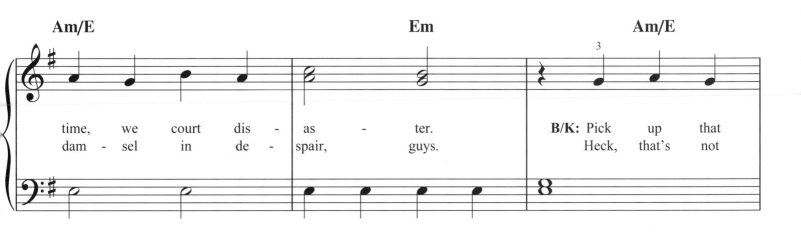

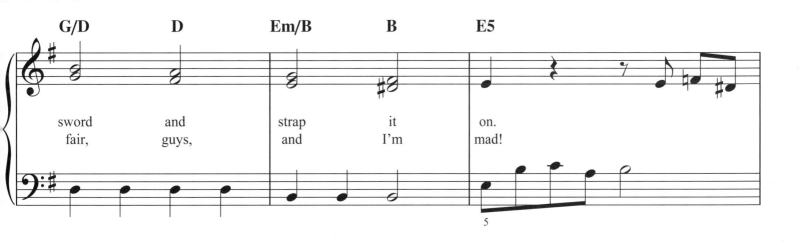

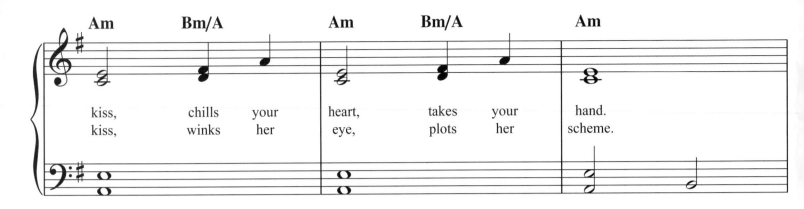

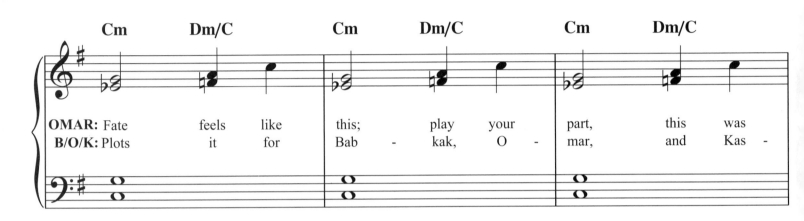

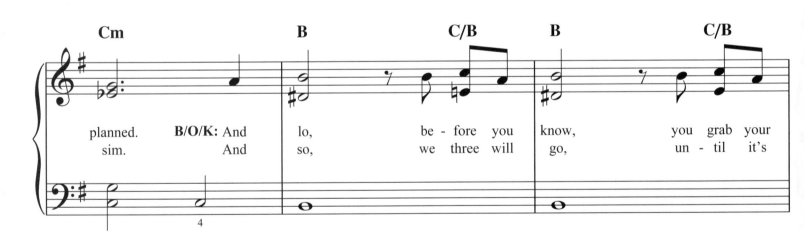

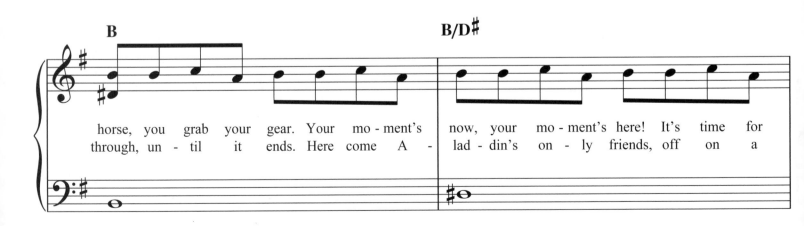

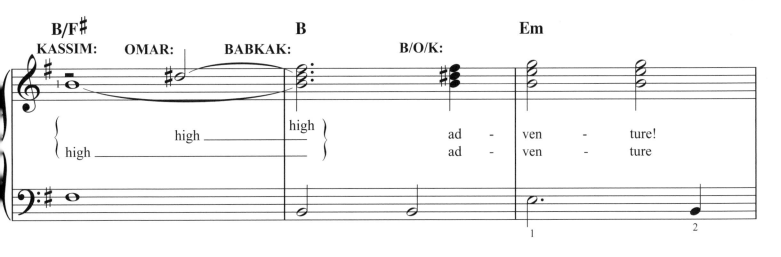

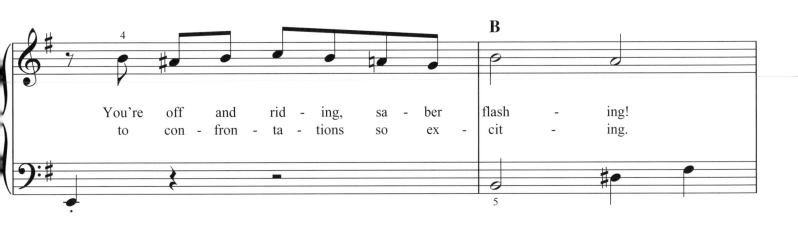

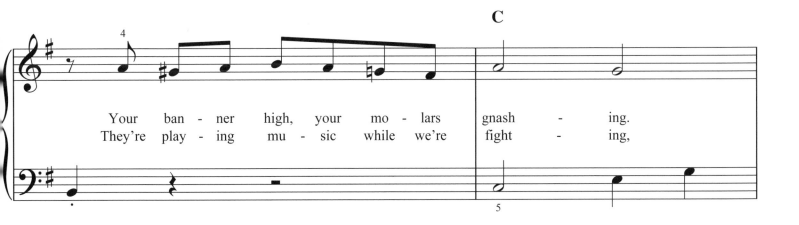

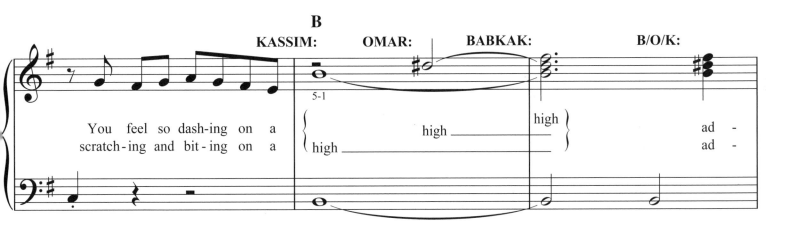

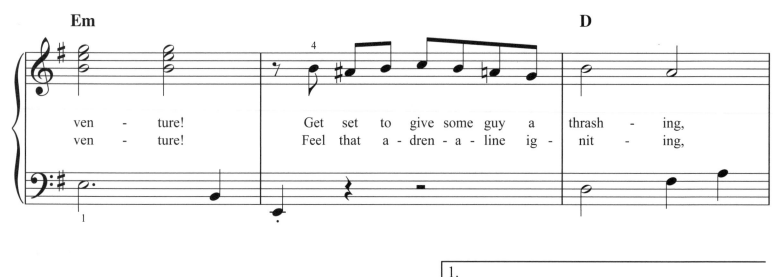

ven - ture! Get set to give some guy a thrash - ing,
ven - ture! Feel that a - dren - a - line ig - nit - ing,

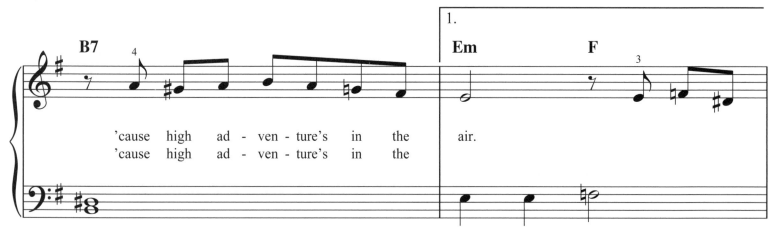

'cause high ad - ven - ture's in the air.
'cause high ad - ven - ture's in the

'cause high ad - ven - ture's in the

air.

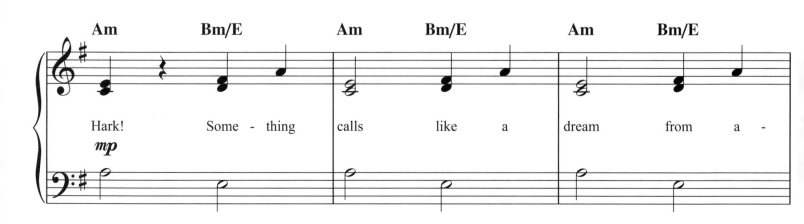

Hark! Some - thing calls like a dream from a -

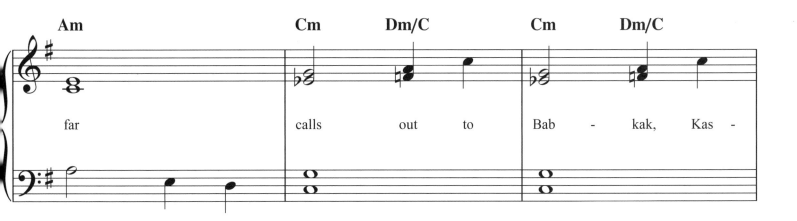

far

calls   out   to   Bab - kak,   Kas -

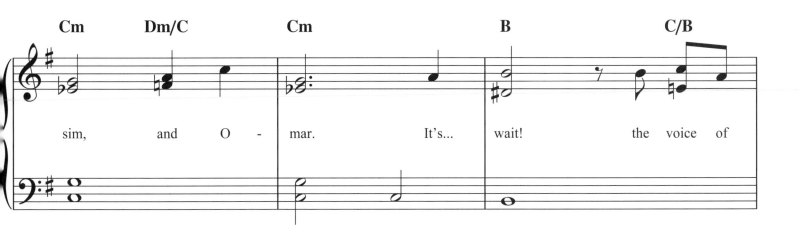

sim,   and   O -   mar.   It's...   wait!   the   voice   of

fate.   It   calls   to   me,   it   calls   to   you,   here   comes   A -

cresc.

lad - din's mot - ley crew.   *f*   It's   time   for   { high _____

                                                                                                            { high _____

KASSIM: OMAR:

2

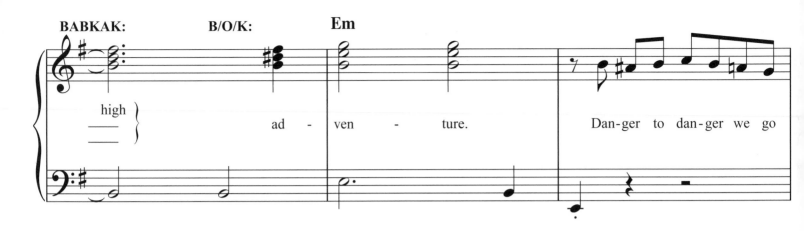

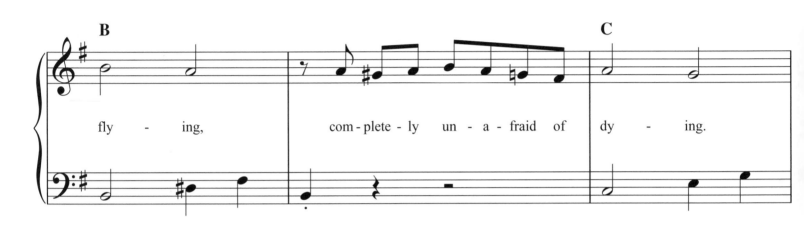

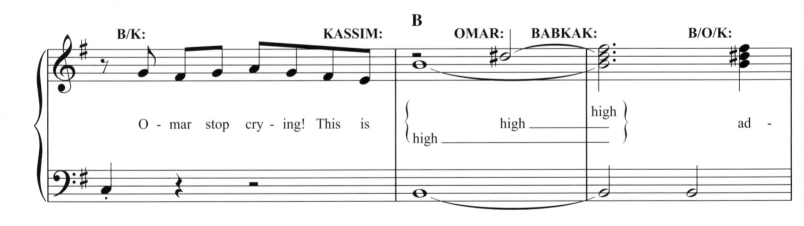

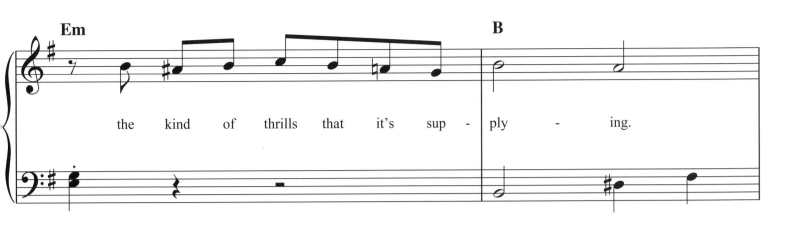

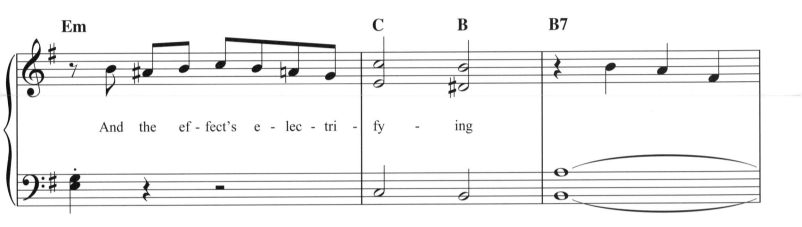

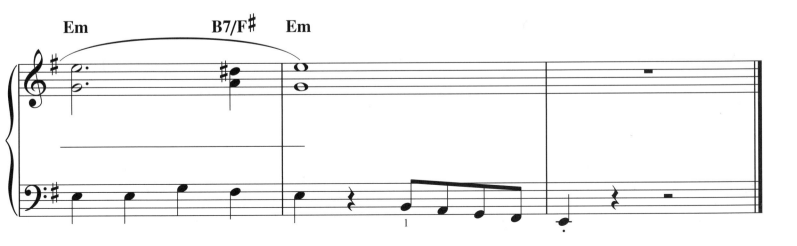

SOMEBODY'S GOT YOUR BACK

Music by ALAN MENKEN
Lyrics by CHAD BEGUELIN

As a teen-y Ge-nie, I would dare to dream

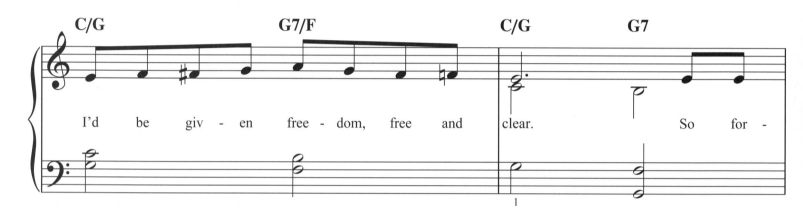

I'd be giv-en free-dom, free and clear. So for-

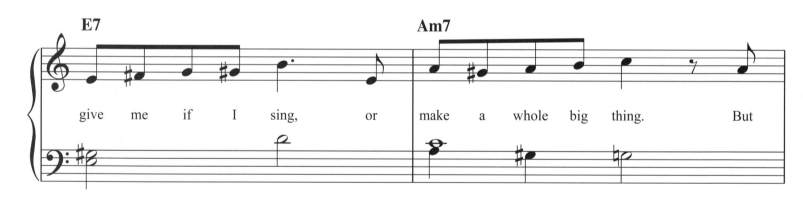

give me if I sing, or make a whole big thing. But

I just can't main-tain my cool ve-neer.

Fats Waller Swing (♪♪ = 3 ♪♪)

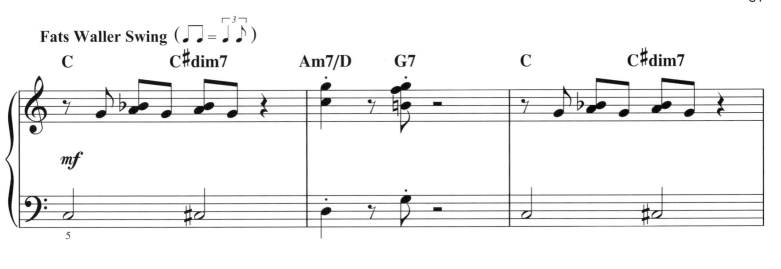

ALADDIN:

You save me, then I'll save you.

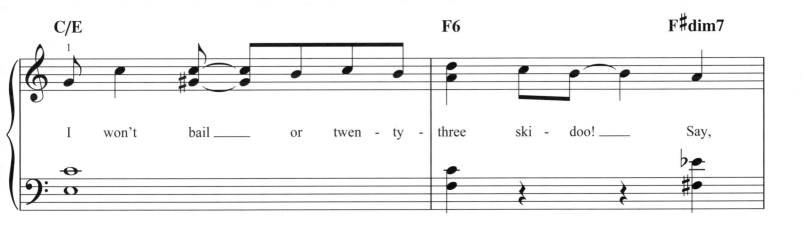

I won't bail ____ or twen - ty - three ski - doo! ____ Say,

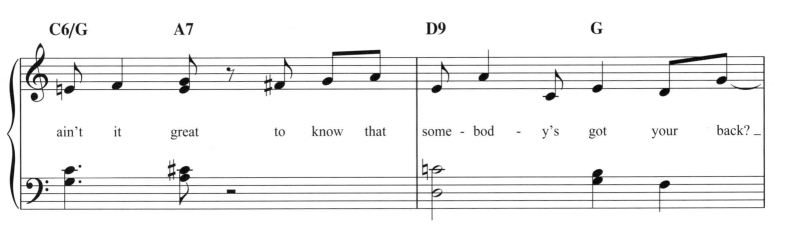

ain't it great to know that some - bod - y's got your back?

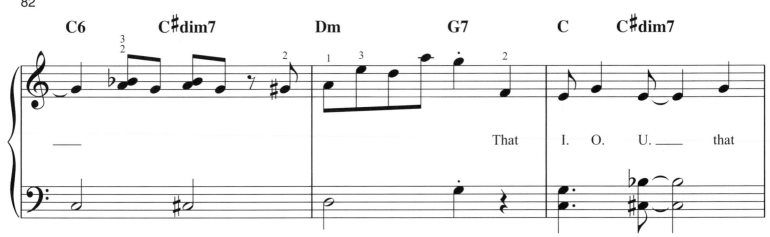

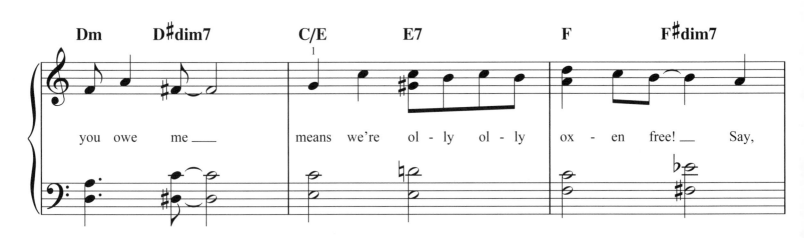

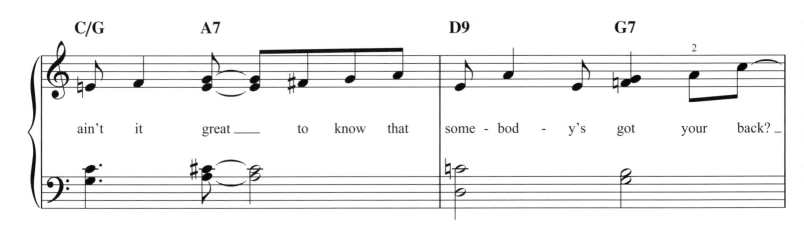

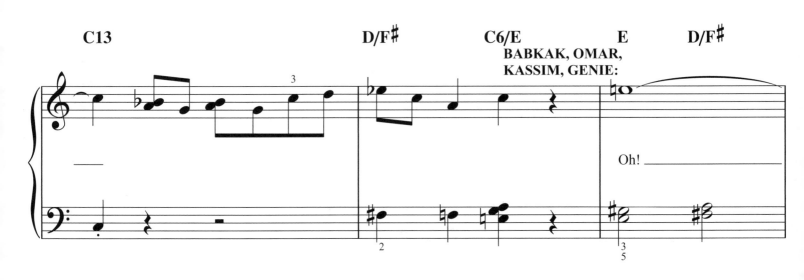

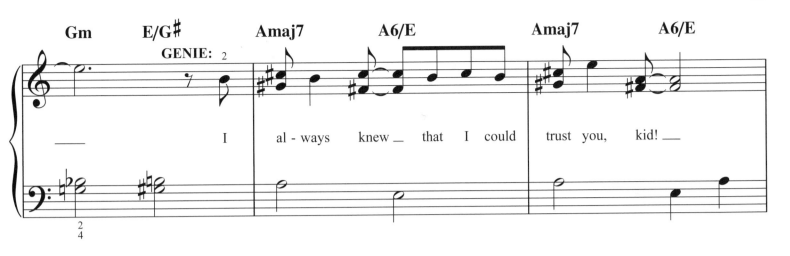

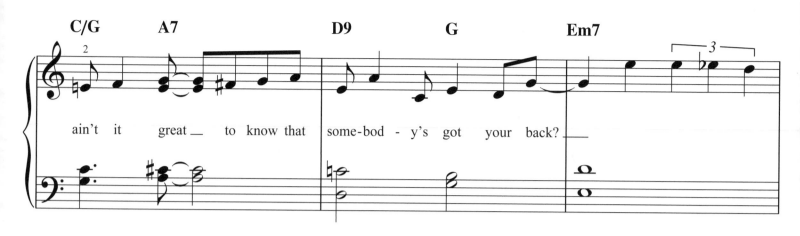

ain't it great __ to know that some-bod - y's got your back? __

Say, ain't it great __ to know some-bod - y's got your back! __

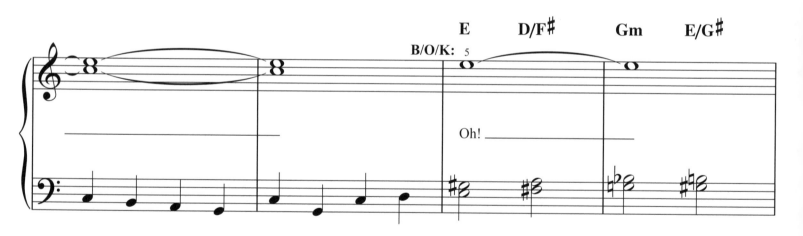

B/O/K:
Oh! _____

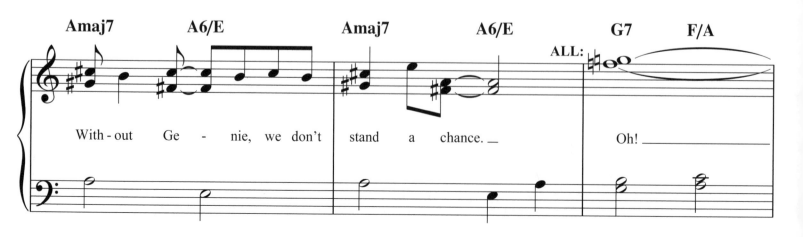

With - out Ge - nie, we don't stand a chance. __

ALL:
Oh! _____

ALADDIN, GENIE: 2

_____ This is the start of a fine bro - mance! Our

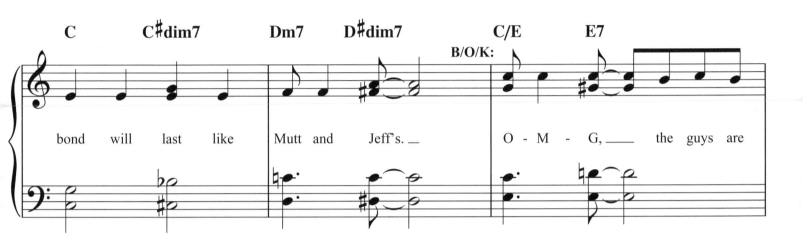

B/O/K:

bond will last like Mutt and Jeff's. _ O - M - G, ___ the guys are

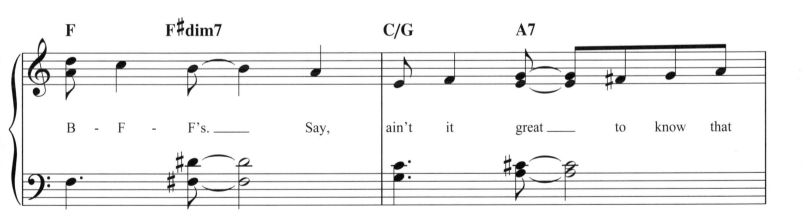

B - F - F's. ___ Say, ain't it great ___ to know that

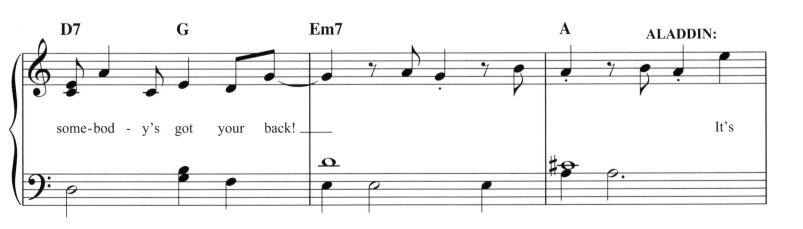

ALADDIN:

some-bod - y's got your back! ___ It's

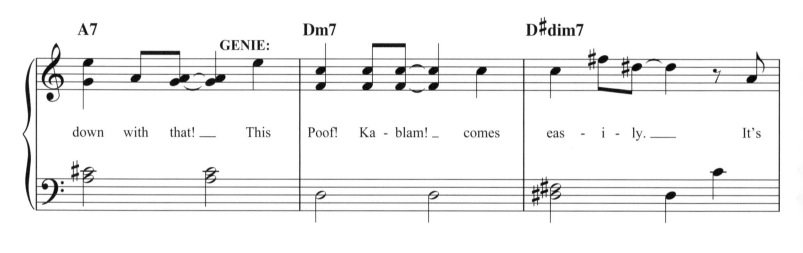

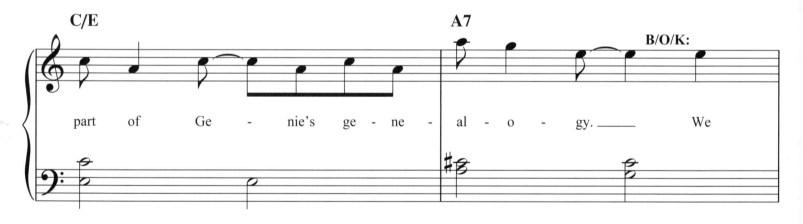

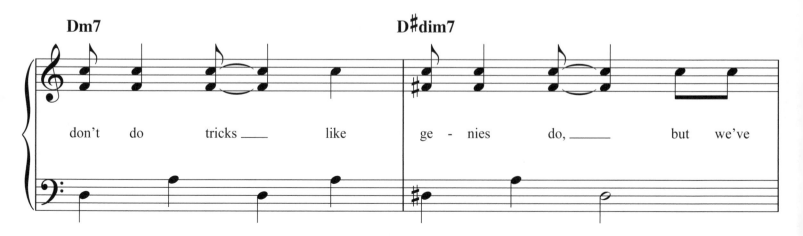

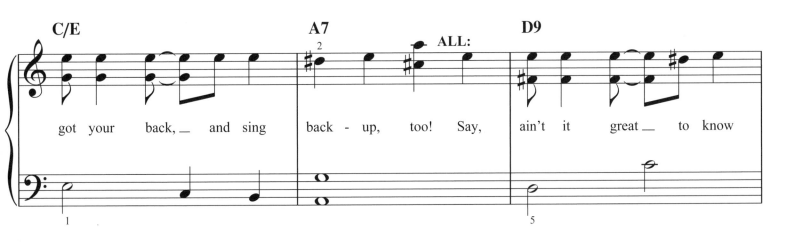

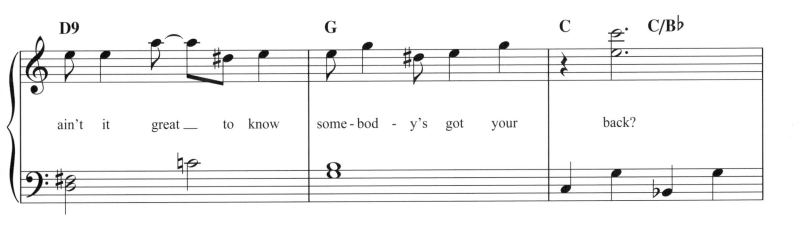

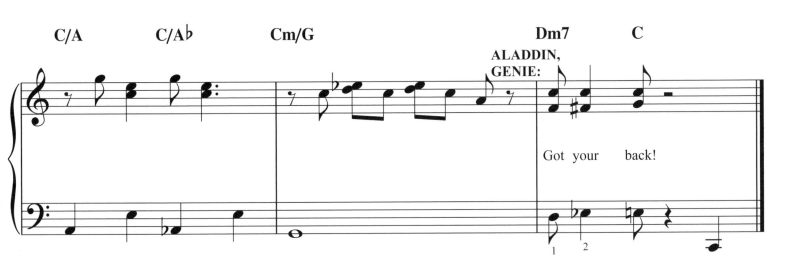